JEWELLERY REPAIRS
At The Bench

Andrew Berry

JEWELLERY REPAIRS

At The Bench

THE CROWOOD PRESS

CONTENTS

Foreword by Charles Lewton-Brain   7

Introduction   9

1   Tools and Equipment   15

2   Materials   29

3   Repairing Chains   35

4   Resizing and Repairing Rings   45

5   Attaching and Repairing Clasps   81

6   Repairing Earrings   85

7   Repairing Bracelets   91

8   Miscellaneous Repairs   103

9   Cleaning, Polishing and Restoring Surfaces and Textures   111

10   Taking In and Collecting Repairs   123

Appendix: Ring Size Conversion Chart   131

Mohs Scale of Hardness   133

Facetted Gemstone Terminology   133

Metal Thickness Conversion   134

Gemstone Vulnerability Table   135

Torts of Interference Act   136

Suppliers   137

Glossary   139

Index   142

FOREWORD

Andrew Berry brings his many years of UK trade and teaching work to this excellent text. This book is written in the spoken voice - authentic and true and real. The voice of experience. It is a privilege to write of Andrew's contributions to the world of jewellery education, and its importance to the field in our time. Repair books have been rare in the last fifty years, and Andrew has written a solid work, of meaning to the future as well as today. A real window into the professional world of jewellery repairing. He starts by talking about the trust that is essential in the jeweller-client relationship. And the idea that repair and maintenance are part of the responsibility of the jewellery owner - all true and rarely mentioned.

His contributions to the field, driven by his understanding of the reduction of education in the field and a personal desire to pass on the knowledge he gathered over his career are many and vital to the revitalization of our field. He has been the gateway, the doorway into jewellery making for many thousands of people. His videos have opened the world of jewellery to so many. He is down to earth and has trade experience (oh so important to the quality of information!) and knows how to communicate with people. And his words are wisdom for aspiring jewellers and repair people.

This book teaches the important things to think about and know when considering jewellery repair. This is the information a skilled goldsmith will use to evaluate, make decisions and perform repairs. Andrew has the best teacher's trick of saying what you think as you make the hundreds of decisions necessary to making and repairing jewellery. A great book. An essential for a serious goldsmith and bench worker.

He begins with a good chapter on health and safety. And superb thorough descriptions of the tools and equipment needed for jewellery repair. There is a rare and welcome section on metals reclamation. Every section is loaded with useful information. The chapters on chain repair go into detail not found in other books. There is a good section on working with platinum. Ring sizing and repairs of all kinds are very well addressed. Andrew is a man who has done a *lot* of repairs. Claw retipping is exhaustively dealt with. Every kind of repair you are likely to run into is discussed thoroughly - a professional training text.

There is a great chapter on how to take in a repair, analyze what is there, the language and customer relations necessary. System management for tracking and tons more on the business side of repairing jewellery is discussed. There are some model documents and a short biography of Andrew. A historically important and excellent book.

Charles Lewton-Brain, Autumn 2025

INTRODUCTION

Jewellery plays an important role in most people's lives. That christening bangle, a communion cross, a signet ring for your coming of age, a friendship ring, engagement ring, wedding ring, eternity ring. All of these items become part of their owner, and over time, naturally begin to show signs of wear and require maintenance.

Perhaps the stone is lost from a ring, or a pet jumping up breaks a chain. You don't just throw these treasured possessions away; you want to get them repaired, as they have both sentimental and monetary worth. Obviously, we are able to check on the condition as time passes, and can often attend to a weak link or loose stone before the inevitable happens. After all, prevention is better than cure, as they say.

Repairs are trust-based. The public will always go to a jeweller who they know and trust. Perhaps the jeweller has sold items or services previously to that person or they have been commissioned to make a personal piece of jewellery. The public will often return to this jeweller rather than go to someone they don't know, even if that person offers repairs at a cheaper price.

So you see, every day, people need their jewellery maintained: it makes complete sense to offer these services in addition to your jewellery-making business. If you have the skills to make jewellery, then you possess the skills to repair jewellery. You may not have the confidence at the beginning, but the more jewellery you work on the more your confidence will grow.

In the beginning, don't be afraid to say no to a repair if you're unsure of how to do it or you don't have the correct equipment. It is better to say no than to attempt the repair, only to run into issues that you're not able to resolve and end up having to explain the problem to the customer. It is important to know your limits and never be afraid to say no.

Obviously, the more time you spend making jewellery, the more confidence you will gain. This is vital, as half the battle when it comes to jewellery repairs is not just the act of repairing, but the analysis of the item way before any work is undertaken on it. You have to play the part of a jewellery detective. The use of magnification is essential to study the item. You should have a basic understanding of jewellery construction, both handmade and mass-produced to spot the construction method of the item. You also need to look for any areas of weakness and essentially, missing gemstones. These may be missing and the space where they were, filled with dirt.

Pay particular attention to the area in need of repair. For instance, if you need to replace a stone, has the claw worn down or is it missing? Have stones near to the one that needs to be replaced had any attention, such as new or built-up claws/prongs? If the ring needs to be resized, has it been resized before? Is it so thin that it is unworkable? Would a new shank be more beneficial? What you don't want to do is start work and then find that previous repairs come undone, or worse still, make your repair unsuccessful.

Above all, you have to remember that you are being entrusted with a client's treasured possession, perhaps an heirloom. Treat it with the respect it deserves. Handle it with care and make sure it is safe when in your possession.

OPPOSITE: Soldering a ring.

HEALTH, SAFETY AND PERSONAL ATTIRE

Workshop Policy

Health and Safety is an ongoing process. You don't think of it once and then forget about it. It is a policy that evolves and develops. We all want to focus on what we love to do but there are a few important aspects that will make your workspace and environment safe to work in. We sometimes forget the safety aspects, and perhaps we will rush or not hold something properly because we want to get the job done. If we start to put a policy in place right at the beginning, we can build on it gradually and it will not be such an intense undertaking later on.

There are some particular areas of a policy that need to be universally addressed and may be more important to some than others; perhaps you have asthma and need to use a more specialised mask, for instance. If you do have a medical condition then it is important to consult a doctor and get a professional opinion. Do not simply rely on friends or forums for help when it comes to health matters. If you are unsure about a particular process or chemical then please take time to learn about it.

First Aid Kit

This is an essential item. Make sure everything in it is in date and well stocked. Keep it near to the bench. Include eye wash just in case anything happens to get in your eye.

First aid kit. This must be compliant with your country's regulations.

The Torch

So let's start off with the obvious item when it comes to soldering. The small hand-held torches are nice and straightforward to use and operate, as there is no setting up required, but if you are using a different type of torch with various fittings, then it's best to consult with an industry professional for advice. As we are going to be working with naked flames we need to have a bucket of sand, appropriate fire extinguishers and also a fire blanket. Please consult a fire protection company for advice. It is important that your soldering areas are fire resistant, with soldering boards on the base. Years ago, I built a soldering station made from four 300 × 300mm, 9mm-thick soldering boards. This is an ideal area to solder, anneal and melt down metal, as it is contained. It is small enough to carry to your bench if you wish or can be left on a dedicated bench.

Apron

Since day one, I've worn an apron and sometimes a lab coat while I'm in the workshop. I feel naked without one. It can be a simple cotton bib apron or the more robust leather types. Why? For several reasons. I like my clothes and whether I wear an old pair of jeans and T-shirt or smart trousers and shirt, I like to protect them from the dirt, dust and sometimes the splashes of liquid at the bench. Also, it gives you a chance to advertise your brand when taking those work-in-progress photos for social media. An apron is also invaluable for when you are sitting at your bench and you drop something; your apron usually catches it instead of the item dropping on the floor and you having to spend ages on your hands and knees looking for it.

Safety Glasses

I have several pairs scattered around the workshop. They should be worn whenever there is a chance of something going in your eye. So, for example, when working with your torch, working with fluids, or when you are polishing. Have them by the equipment you need them for, so there's no excuse. Invest in a pair of welder's glasses to protect your eyes when you're melting metal.

Ear Protection

If you are carrying out excessive hammering then ear protection is a must. We won't be undertaking hammering

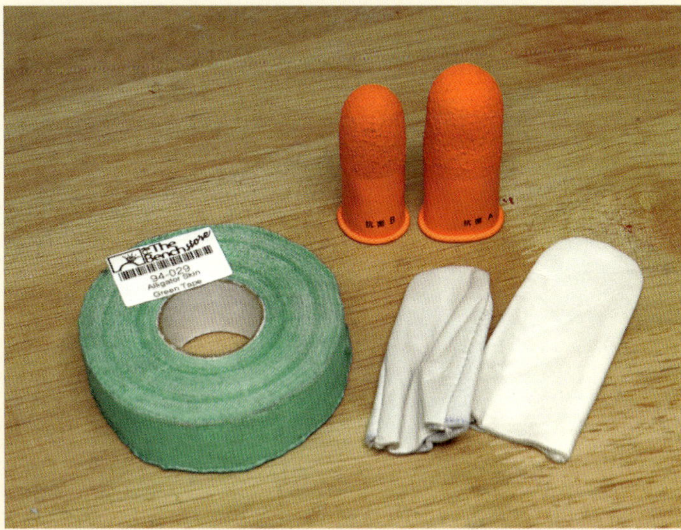
Various types of protection for your fingers.

Finger cots

Often made from latex and rubber. The latex type will keep your hands clean but they will not offer any protection. The rubber type are available in three sizes and offer a certain amount of protection, but being rubber, they can easily be worn away.

Leather protectors

These are available for the thumb and finger. They tend to be quite thick so you do not have much feeling through the leather.

Gloves

These are not often used as the latex type will wear through easily. Other types of gloves do offer protection but are very dangerous when using rotary equipment such as polishing motors. If the spindle or mop catches the glove it can be ripped off or worse still, your hand can be pulled onto the mop or spindle.

Alligator tape

This is a low-tack tape that sticks to itself. See the photo instructions showing how I use it to protect my fingers.

in this book but some kind of ear protection is important if you are using a polishing motor for any length of time.

Finger Protection

Protecting your fingers from your saw, files and buff sticks and even the heat of the metal when polishing is crucial.

How to use alligator tape

Unroll 100mm of tape.

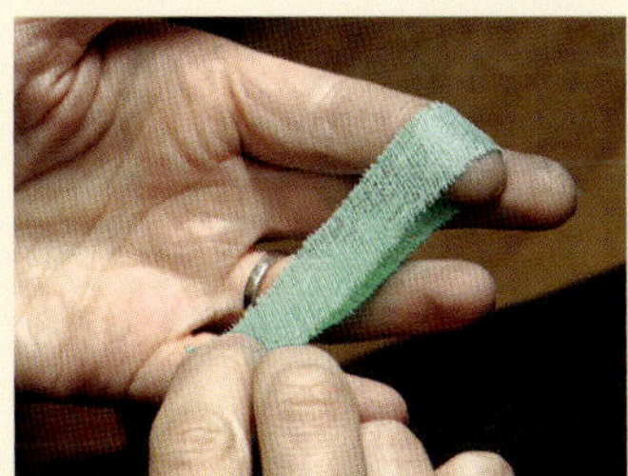
Fold it in half.

Wrap it over the end of your finger or thumb.

Put tape on the folded-over piece.

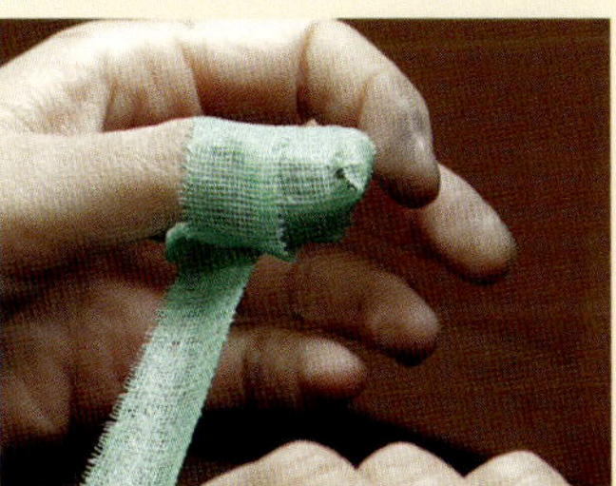
Wrap it around several times.

You can also wrap it over the end to offer a bit more protection.

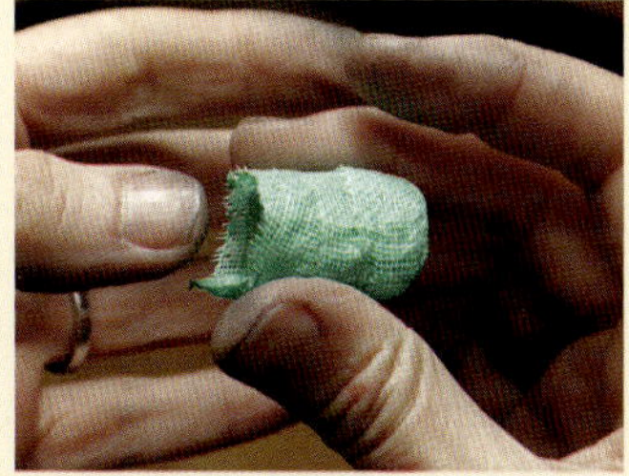
If you have not wrapped it too tight, you can take it off and put it on again.

Breathing Protection

Most jewellery-making processes can cause some form of dust and a lot of it becomes airborne. We don't want to breathe it in so a simple fabric mask with a filter should be the basic minimum. If you are polishing then a mask with a particle filter would be advantageous. Ensuring that there is no dust lying around also helps – a clean workshop is a happy workshop.

Clothing

If you wear long-sleeved shirts, make sure the cuffs are buttoned or the sleeves are rolled up. Make sure that they are not too baggy in case they get caught or flap in front of a flame.

Shoes

Never wear open-toed sandals in the workshop. There are lots of heavy tools and equipment and you don't want anything falling on your toes. Always wear sensible shoes and not light canvas shoes.

Personal

If you have long hair, please tie it back out of the way. Jewellery such as large rings or dangling chains should not be worn in the workshop as all these are hazards. Keep lanyards tucked in. If retrieving an item from the floor when polishing, turn the motor off before bending down to pick it up.

Chemicals and Fluids

All fluids and chemicals should be kept in a lockable cupboard and every container should be labelled. Make sure you are familiar with the instructions and what the chemicals and fluids are and do. Keep a box of disposable gloves in the cupboard as you should always protect your hands when handling potentially harmful fluids.

You should always dispose of used chemicals and fluids correctly. Have a chat with your local government recycling centre for the best advice on how to dispose. *Never* pour anything down the sink or drains.

Fire Extinguishers and Smoke Alarms

It is essential when working with naked flames to be very careful and aware of your surroundings. Make sure you have a safe area to work in, with a heatproof surface. Have a small fire extinguisher right next to your soldering area or a

Good lighting is essential; overall lighting and also a good bench light.

bucket of damp sand just in case anything happens to catch fire. It is important to have equipment serviced every year.

There are a few types of fire extinguishers that you will need:

Powder (blue) – This is safe to use on wood, paper, textiles, live electrical fires and flammable liquids.

CO2 (black) – This can be used on flammable liquids, live electrical fires but not on wood, paper and textiles.

Water (red) – This is safe to use on wood, paper, textiles but not for live electrical equipment and flammable liquids.

Smoke alarms are also required but don't position them right above where you are working with a flame, as you'll find it going off every time you light up the torch. Position it away from your bench and make sure you change the batteries on a regular basis.

Lighting

Although good lighting is very important when making jewellery, a dimly lit area for soldering enables you to work more efficiently, as you will be able to see the metal change colour as it's heated. We have general room lighting from a ceiling light and then a more concentrated task light over the bench area where we are working. A light directly over the bench is important when setting items up to be soldered, but then the ability to turn it off is advantageous.

Precious Metal Reclamation

Keeping the workshop clean and tidy is so important when working with precious metals, gemstones and diamonds. Inevitably you will drop metal or stones onto the floor and they are easier to see with a clean, dust free floor. The action of polishing precious metals creates dust from the polishing mops and this dust will contain minute specks of precious metals so it pays to wipe every surface, sweep the floor and retain all this dust along with wipes in a special plastic bag: your sweeps bag.

It's not just the dust you need to keep. You need to keep everything, such as old mops, emery paper – even if it's worn out. If you have extraction on your polishing motor then you need to clean out the filters and put that dust in your sweeps bag. This will also help to ensure your motor runs efficiently too.

Wipe your hands with wet wipes before you wash them in the sink, this will help catch the small particles of precious metal dust trapped in your hands. Also wipe your bench down from time to time, putting all wipes into your sweeps bag.

Try to use carpets in your workshop. The carpet will help trap the precious metal dust and stop it walking out of the workshop on your shoes. If a carpet is not possible then a hard floor that you can wipe over with a damp floor mop is good, again putting the floor wipe in the bag. Where carpets are used ensure they do not pose a trip hazard.

Before you go home of an evening, hoover your clothes and apron and even your apron pockets. When the vacuum bag is full, put the contents in your sweeps bag.

You can purchase settlement tanks, which are placed under a sink and connected to the waste pipe. The idea is that as metal dust is heavier than water, the separate chambers in the settlement tank trap the metal dust and the sludge that gets trapped is collected by a precious metal reclamation company. We had a couple of these tanks but found that even after five years there was hardly any metal dust collected due to the efficient dust collection in our workshop.

Your ultrasonic bath should not be ignored. Before you come to change the solution, let it settle for a day or so, then carefully drain the water off leaving the sludge in the bottom. Use a few pieces of kitchen roll to wipe the bottom of the tank and put that wipe in the sweeps bag.

So as you can see, over a period of time all of this dust and sludge adds up and a precious metal reclamation company will be able to collect it, refine it and buy the precious metal it contains. This could amount to hundreds if not thousands of pounds over the years. Dust and sludge you may have otherwise simply thrown out.

Lemel

This is the fine metal dust that is created when you file and saw metal. This dust should be collected but kept separate from your sweeps bag, it should have its own collection pot as the lemel is of a higher grade than the sweepings. You can keep the lemel in separate containers for each metal, or you can simply collect it in one pot. The precious metal reclamation companies can determine the quality of the lemel once it has been melted, and you will get paid based upon the quality of the metal.

Keep a thick bag to put all of your emery paper and floor sweepings into. The paper towels from when you wipe the workshop down go in here and also the paper towels after you clean the ultrasonic.

The filings that come off your metal and onto your bench all get swept into a lemel pot.

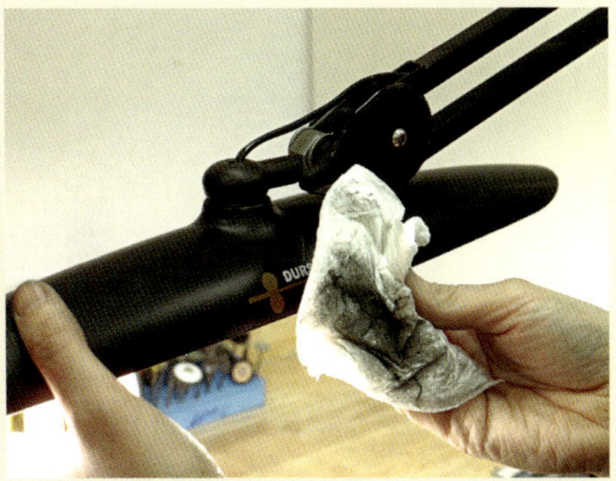

There is dust and dirt everywhere in the workshop and it has some precious metal in it, so it pays to wipe everything down weekly with a moist paper towel.

CHAPTER 1

TOOLS AND EQUIPMENT

The advantage with carrying out jewellery repairs is that you do not need an awful lot of tools or equipment. Simple repairs can be carried out with basic equipment, which means it's an inexpensive way to start making money. If you are already making jewellery whether it be silver or gold, you should have most of the tools and equipment needed to repair jewellery. Over the next few pages, we will be looking at the equipment that I use. There are one or two specialist pieces of equipment available to make your life a little bit easier, and the cost of these tools pays for itself tenfold. You do not necessarily need these at the start but they will make your life easier and get the job done more quickly.

You may have already been making jewellery for a while, in which case you may have a dedicated space, workshop or studio. Having a separate area is beneficial, especially when you start to buy specialist equipment – often larger items that need to be fastened down to shelves or worktops. However, simply working at your dining table doing the most basic repairs is a great way to start building up your confidence, enabling you to buy more tools to make repairs that little bit easier.

Everything in the Hand Tool section you should already have as staple workshop tools if you are regularly making jewellery. The items in the Workshop Tools section are not a necessity but are great to have, as they will help with efficiency when it comes to repairs.

WORKBENCHES

Whilst it is always nice having a dedicated table or better still, a jeweller's bench, to work at, you really don't need one for starting out with jewellery repairs. Any sturdy table or worktop is going to be suitable. Obviously, you don't want to be using your dining table as it is going to get dirty, marked and possibly burnt. A sturdy work surface is the bare minimum. If you go down that route then all you will need is a bench anvil and peg, more information on which is in the next section.

Fitted bench peg.

OPPOSITE: Wearing the appropriate safety equipment.

If space and money allow, then it is always best to have a dedicated jeweller's bench. There are many different types to choose from, starting with an inexpensive student bench right up to a professional model. The one thing they all have in common is a slight curved front that allows you to sit closer to the work surface. If you place a tray (or a skin as it's originally known), beneath the bench peg area, you will be able to catch the filings and lemel as you work. This 'dust' is swept up daily and placed in small containers and when you have enough you can send it off to a precious metal reclamation specialist who will process the dust and pay you for the precious metal contained in it.

HAND TOOLS

Bench Anvil and Peg

If you don't have a purpose-made jeweller's bench that has a fitting for a bench peg, an anvil is fastened onto a table or bench and you can attach a wooden jeweller's peg/pin, which for me, is the centre of my universe when sitting at the bench. The advantage of a clamp-on bench peg is that there is usually a flat anvil area, which is useful to tap things flat and straight.

Bench pegs are often the same basic shape but are available in slightly different dimensions. When you buy the bench anvil, a bench peg is supplied so you shouldn't have to buy another one for a while, but if you need to replace it make sure you buy one that fits.

When the peg is new, jewellers often cut a small V out of the front of the peg. This is for supporting your work whilst you cut and file it, which makes working with rings and the like easier and helps you work more efficiently.

Saw

There are many designs available but buying the most expensive saw frame will not help improve your piercing/sawing. Buy an inexpensive model. I prefer a fixed frame saw; there is less to go wrong with it, it's lighter to use, and it is the most basic. I still have the first saw I bought over 38 years ago and I still use it to this day.

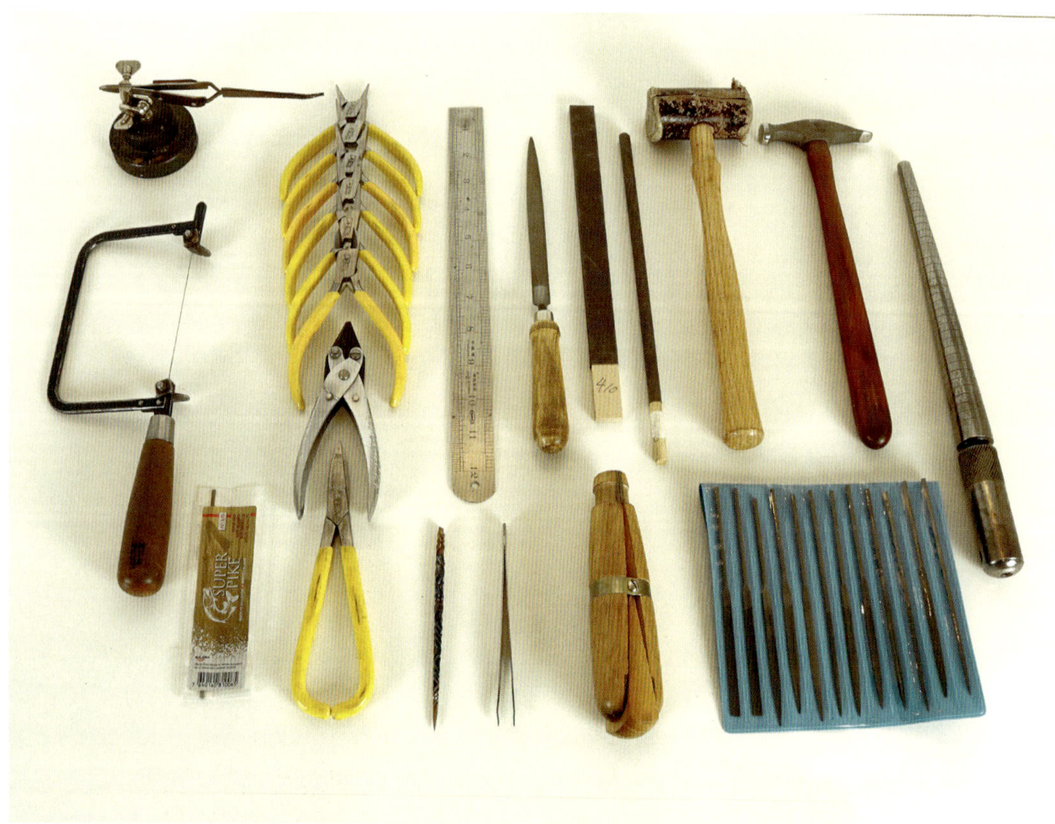

Assorted tools.

Blades

With so many blade brands on the market it seems impossible to choose which one is best. In my career I have tried all the brands and have settled on just one particular brand and size of blade, but as long as you buy blades from a trusted supplier and a trusted brand then you should have no problems. There are around twelve different sizes of blades, usually used for different thicknesses of metal. I simply keep a size 3/0 in my saw at all times. I buy my blades by the gross (12 dozen, 144 blades), this way they work out cheaper in the long run.

Also make use of lubrication when sawing. There is special wax designed for lubricating saws and burrs and whilst this is excellent, you can also use beeswax or even candle wax.

Mallet

This can be made from leather, plastic or rubber. I have always used a rawhide mallet. This mallet is different from a hammer because the mallet doesn't mark the metal as you hit it, it simply forms it without leaving any dents like a metal hammer would. When you buy a new rawhide mallet, the varnish on the leather can be a little bit hard. To 'soften' up the head a little it needs to be conditioned. This can be achieved by hitting the mallet face against a concrete wall or paving slab to soften it. Just make sure that there are no small pieces of concrete or stones embedded in the face of the mallet afterwards.

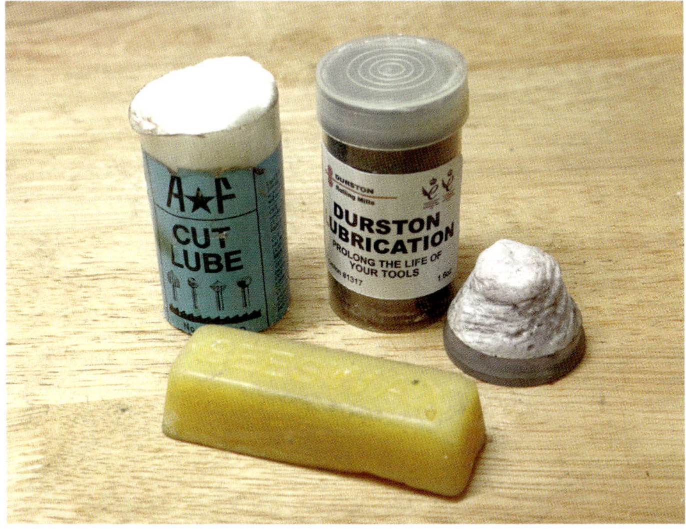

Various lubrication for saw blades.

Pliers

There are several types of pliers used in jewellery making and it can be confusing which ones to buy. Start off looking for a box joint construction as opposed to a lap joint. The box joints are a lot stronger and harder wearing. I still have a few pliers that I bought over twenty years ago and they're still going strong. You can buy them with leaf springs in the handles but I tend to remove them if I buy a pair with them in. I like to feel the pliers as I am using them and if the handles are being forced open all the time it can get very tiring on the hands.

Flat-nose pliers – As the name implies, these pliers have flat faces and wide jaws and are used for holding and bending metal. You can hold small items in the jaws when you have to file or cut them.

Snipe-nose pliers – The ends of these pliers taper and the faces of the jaws are flat. They are similar in appearance to the round-nose pliers. These are great for bending and shaping metal and getting into the tight areas that flat-nosed pliers would not fit. These pliers are also called chain-nose pliers.

Round-nose pliers – The jaws of these pliers are completely round and tapered towards the end. These are used for turning wire into tight curves, making coils or for making the occasional jump ring.

Half-round pliers – One jaw is flat, the other is half-round in section. These pliers are used every time you resize a ring as the curved jaw prevents marks being put into the metal when bending it into a gentle curve.

Parallel pliers – Parallel pliers are available as snipe-nose and standard-nose pliers. What makes parallel pliers special is that the jaws close parallel with each other whereas normal pliers come together in a scissor action. This ensures that there is uniform pressure exerted along the length of the jaws making the grip more secure.

Cutters

Available as side cutters or end cutters, these are used for cutting wire quickly and easily. The cut ends are not always flush so some tidying up of the ends is necessary.

Shears

Shears look like a pair of scissors. They are designed for shearing (cutting) metal. A small narrow pair is the best to buy because we are going to be primarily using them to cut small pieces of solder, called 'pallions'. Smaller and narrower jaws can cut smaller pallions of solder.

Ring File

There are plenty of files available but a great one to start with does the job of two files so it makes sense to buy this file as your first. A ring file tapers to a point, and one side of the file is flat and the other is slightly rounded. So why, I hear you saying, is it called a ring file? Well, because you use it primarily on rings. If you need to file the inside of the ring you would use the rounded side of the file and then when you need to file the outside of the ring then you flip the file over and use the flat side. It is quicker using this type of file because you don't have to put one file down and then pick another up.

Handles

Handles on files are important to have. Some jewellers use files without handles. The tang that usually goes into the handle is long and pointed. If you catch the file and it stops quickly, there is a good chance that your arm will continue moving forward and that sharp tang gets dug into the heel of your hand and you are out of action until that heals. Handles are inexpensive and it only takes a matter of minutes to fit, so please make sure that you have handles on your files for comfort and safety.

Needle Files

As the name suggests, these files are smaller than regular files and come in all shapes. Buying a student set of around 6 or 12 shapes will last you many years and is better value than buying them individually.

Ring Clamps

There are several styles available which all do the same thing: hold rings and other small items in the leather-lined jaws. I prefer the wedge type of clamp because my hand can grip all the way round the clamp. If I use the wing nut style, the nut gets in the way of my hand and grasp on the clamp.

Ruler

This is usually a steel rule and can be 150mm (6 inches) or 300mm (12 inches). Try not to use plastic rulers as they can get marked and pick up little shavings or metal dust that become embedded in the plastic and scratch your work.

Scribe

This can be a commercially available one or a simple sharpened nail. As long as it has a narrow sharp point then that's good enough.

Emery Sticks

There are commercially available emery/buff sticks but over the past 35 years of being a professional jeweller, I have always liked to make my own. Call it lazy or call it being efficient, but I only make a couple of emery sticks with the same grade paper on them: 600-grit. A commercial set contains varying grades of emery sticks. The idea is that you start with the roughest and use it to smooth the surface of the metal down, going through each grade of emery stick until you have a very smooth fine surface. Whilst this is a good method, I find that it is the slowest and for me, time is money.

So this is what I do: I use 600-grit on both emery sticks and make them up as shown. Now, when you use the sticks you wear down the paper and as you wear it down the grit gets finer. Which means on one stick you now have a rough new grit and on the other side you have a slightly finer worn grit. That means we effectively have two emery sticks in one and we just need to flip it over to use the rough or smooth side. The same goes for the second emery stick I have. I have two emery sticks with 4 faces all of varying degrees of grit, so now I can work faster and more effectively as I don't have to put down a stick and look for the next finest, then put that one down, well, you get the idea.

The only exception to this is when working with platinum, as it is such a hard metal. Every stage of buffing is necessary in this case, working down the grits sequentially, and keeping dedicated tools for platinum to avoid cross-contamination of metal.

Making your own buff sticks

Making a buff stick – using wooden stick, choice of emery paper, cutting mat, tape and scorer.

Place the stick on the emery paper, lined up with one edge. Score along the stick edge.

Turn the stick onto its narrow edge, and keeping the previous score in alignment with its guiding edge, score another line to outline the narrow edge.

Turn again, and score to outline the wide edge.

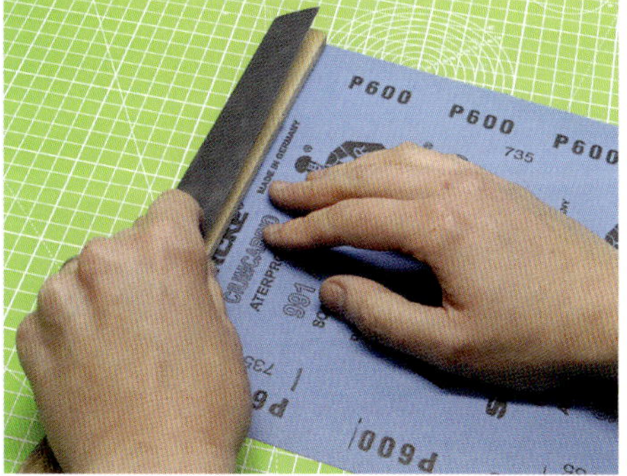

Fold the emery paper over the stick, sharpening the creases to neaten.

Fold and score one more time, then carefully fold over the remaining emery paper.

Remove excess.

Add tape to top and bottom to secure the emery paper.

The finished buff stick.

Tweezers

You simply cannot have too many pairs of tweezers when it comes to jewellery making or indeed soldering. My favourite tweezers are stainless steel AA (anti-acid) tweezers. There are a few pairs on my bench that I've had for years. They benefit from the occasional cleaning and straightening up to keep them efficient. You will use tweezers a lot and you will find that they are cheap enough to have several. I adapt the ends into various sizes of points depending on what I want them to do.

Reverse action tweezers on a base

Reverse action means when you squeeze the tweezers they don't close, they open and spring closed. The tweezers are available with insulated handles and also with straight or bent tips. It really doesn't matter which type you use. They are articulated and attached to a weighted base, often together called a third hand, although they can be bought separately. The third hand can be positioned next to your soldering block and the tweezers moved into the right position to enable you to have two hands free whilst soldering.

Brass tweezers

Nice and inexpensive tweezers. I don't often use them, but they are handy for transferring items in and out of safety pickle without spoiling it.

Soldering Surface

Charcoal blocks are the traditional soldering surface but nowadays soldering boards and blocks are the more popular choice. A charcoal block is often used as the surface reflects the heat back onto the item being soldered or heated up, speeding up your work. They do tend to be a bit pricy so jewellers often go for soldering boards and blocks. There are lots of different styles to choose from and each jeweller has their favourite.

Blocks and boards are available in a variety of sizes but I use a 150mm-square (6 inch) soldering board and then I place a rectangular soldering block on top of the board. I solder on top of the block and should anything roll or drop off the block it will land on the solder board and not burn your bench. The board is also useful should you need to anneal wire that is longer than your solder block. The surfaces, over the years, will get dirty from the fluxes and flame but they can be reconditioned by rubbing them on a flat concrete surface to sand them down. This can be carried out several times before the block and boards get too thin.

Safety Pickle

Years ago sulphuric acid was used but nowadays we use safety pickle (sodium bisulphate), which is a lot safer to use but care still needs to be taken when handling and using it. Safety pickle comes as a powder and is mixed with warm water to make a saturated solution. Add the safety pickle until the water cannot dissolve any more.

The pickle works best when it is warm. Pickle pots are commercially available but some people use a small slow cooker with water in it and the pickle in a glass or plastic container in the water, just like a bain-marie. I have always used baby bottle warmers, again with some water in it and the pickle in a jam jar in the water. The water is heated and keeps the pickle warm. Safety pickle is more effective on gold and silver when it is warm.

You must never put anything steel or iron into your pickle as it will contaminate the pickle. You will have to dispose of what you have and make a fresh batch. Stainless steel, brass and copper tweezers are safe to use with pickle.

Magnification

I have always used magnification because if the item I'm repairing looks good under magnification, then it will look amazing without it. Even when I was young I used magnification. I use an Optivisor, a band that goes around your head with a flip-up eye glass in front. These can be obtained in various magnifications. When I am in front of a client I often use a 10× loupe to examine the jewellery, checking all over the item including underneath and inside rings. Stating and recording condition at take-in is important to avoid any potential disputes in the future. It is better to do this now rather than have to contact the client to say there was something else wrong with their jewellery.

Solder blocks and solder pick.

Pickle pot.

Optivisor (magnification).

WORKSHOP TOOLS

Rolling Mill

This was one of the first items I purchased when I started out in business back in the 1980s. I knew that it would pay for itself over and over again and it certainly has. A rolling mill's primary job is to reduce the shape and dimensions of a piece of metal. This means that you won't need to stock many sizes of metal, as the rolling mill can shape the metal for a specific repair. Rolling mills can be geared, non-geared or electric. It really doesn't matter but what you want to look for in a mill is flat rollers for reducing sheet metal, V grooves to reduce square wire and D-section grooves (these can be as extension rolls or built into the main rolls) to reduce square wire into D-section wire.

Having a rolling mill means that you can simply stock one or two sections of metal and make it the correct section and size for a particular job, rather than stocking numerous varieties, some of which you will not use often. This will ensure that money is not tied up in metal when it can be utilised elsewhere.

Pendant Motor/Flex Shaft

A pendant motor, often called a flex shaft, is used for drilling, polishing, texturing and grinding. It is used many times a day and with so many accessories it will be one of your most used items of equipment.

A flex shaft is preferable over a drill like a hand-held Dremel, as it has a removable handpiece, meaning you can swap to a different type such as a hammer-action handpiece. A flex shaft has more torque, meaning it has more power and won't slow down when pressure is applied to the rotating drill or mop. The actual motor is usually suspended above your bench with a flexible shaft running down from it into a handpiece. It is best to get a removable handpiece as opposed to a fixed handpiece. It is usually operated via a foot pedal.

Micro Motor

As the name implies, the motor is smaller and more delicate. It is often used for more delicate drilling operations such as micro and pavé setting, although you can use it for everything that a flex shaft can do – it's just not as robust and heavy duty.

Geared rolling mill.

Motor and flex shaft.

Polishing Motor

The second piece of equipment I bought when I first started in business. I had used one whilst I was in university and knew the advantages. Because of the size of the motor, polishing is quicker and easier, producing a more professional finish than any other method. The motor can be single or double spindle, double being a better option as you can leave the mops on the spindles without having to swap them over for different polishes. They are available with and without extraction. Extraction is a better option although more expensive, but it keeps all the dust in the dust collector instead of it flying around your workshop.

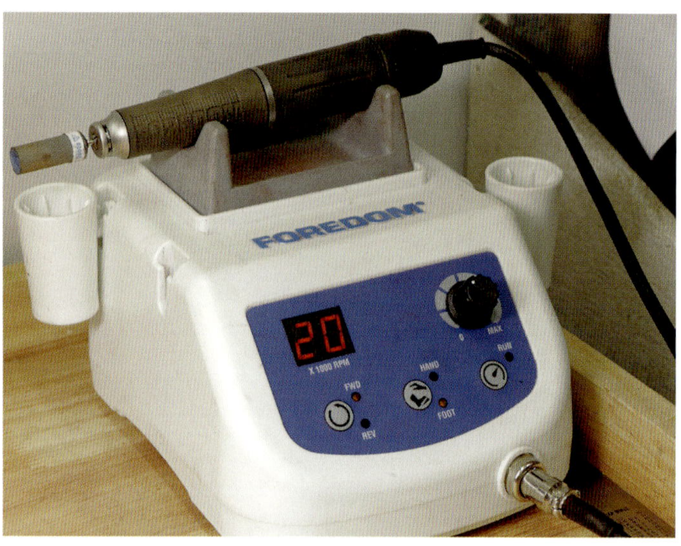
Micro motor.

Double motor polisher.

The extracted dust can be collected and sent to a refiner to recover the minute particles of precious metal that are polished off. *See* Precious Metal Reclamation.

Polishing Mops

Often known as buffing wheels, they are used to polish metal to achieve a smooth high gloss finish with the addition of a polishing compound or jeweller's rouge. The polishing compound is applied to the mop by way of a bar. They are typically made of various materials like cotton, felt, or sisal, and come in different forms, including stitched and loose-leaf. A harder mop is used for pre-polishing and a softer, swansdown, mop should be used with the final polish such as rouge. These mops must always be kept apart and one must never contaminate the other.

Finger Mops

Finger mops are specifically designed for use in tight corners and areas where a larger mop wouldn't reach and are used to polish up the inside of rings. Like mops, you should keep separate finger mops for pre-polish and final polish.

Upright Wedding Ring Enlarger and Reducer

One of the first items of equipment I bought when I moved into my first workshop. I knew that this tool would make me money, as it's a versatile ring sizing machine, enlarging and reducing plain wedding bands, and also engraved

Polishing mops.

bands with care. You can buy these machines with built-in ring shank benders, which is a great money saving tip.

Gem Ring Stretcher

The gem ring stretcher does exactly that. It stretches gem-set rings by rolling the ring shank, enlarging the ring. With the advent of cheap mass-manufactured rings, some ring shanks have been hollowed out for lightness, therefore cost effectiveness. This causes a problem with stretching rings using this piece of equipment as by rolling over hollow areas, you will damage the ring. The best way to enlarge a gem-set ring is to add metal, but if the ring shank is thick enough then a gem ring stretcher can be used to enlarge a size or two without thinning out the shank too much.

Shank Benders

A handy piece of equipment, but not essential. It enables you to bend metal into gentle curves. This is ideal if you are adding a few sizes into a ring and need the thick metal curved to fit the existing profile of the original shank. It is also great to bend metal should the ring need a quarter, half or full shank. There are pliers that will do the same as a shank bender for a fraction of the price so I would consider a shank bender a bit of a luxury item.

Gem ring stretcher and dies.

Shank bender.

Upright ring stretcher.

Ultrasonic Cleaners

Some see ultrasonic cleaners as a luxury, but really, they are essential in every jewellery workshop. They work by immersing the item in a solution of ultrasonic cleaning fluid and water. It works best when heated to around 50°C. The vibration of the ultrasonic waves is sent through the solution and it is these waves that help to dissolve and dislodge the dirt. The dirt and polish on the ring might need a bit of persuading to remove it, if after a few minutes the ring is not clean. You can use a soft toothbrush to gently remove the dirt and polish and then return it back to the ultrasonic solution. The solution needs to be changed each week; this is often done through the drain tap or emptying the tank through a coffee filter to trap any stones that may have been dislodged.

An ultrasonic rack is vital to suspend the jewellery in the solution. Nothing must rest on the base of the tank, as this will cause premature wear, resulting in scratches that distort the ultrasonic waves and as such it will not operate efficiently. If you have concerns about items containing gemstones, use a plastic tea strainer or put the item in a zip-lock bag with a little solution in it. Close the top and drop it into the tank. the waves will pass through the bag and clean the item inside. Note that there are several types of gemstones that should not be placed in an ultrasonic bath; a table illustrating this can be found in the appendix.

Ultrasonic bath.

Barrel Polishers

We don't often use barrel polishers in the repair workshop, as they are unsuitable for gem-set jewellery. The only advantage of a barrel polisher is to barrel chains, as it is just too dangerous to polish with any rotary tool. Do not just throw the chains into the barrel as they are, though. Wrap them around a wire frame or use a hole punch to make a few holes in a piece of flexible plastic and pass the chain through and fasten it. These methods will stop the chains from tangling in the barrel.

Magnetic Polishers

These consist of a barrel of very fine stainless steel pins on top of a box that houses strong rotating earth magnets. As these magnets rotate the pins in the barrel are pulled around in a soapy solution, polishing the items inside the barrel. The units can be small, made for a couple of rings for example, or larger barrels that can take twenty or so rings at a time. Having said all this, these magnetic polishers are not often used in the jewellery repair workshop, more the jewellery manufacturing workshop. They can be beneficial if you have larger items to polish. Depending on the type of pins in the barrel, the finish is often a very fine matte finish, so you would need to either barrel polish the item if it had no stones in it, or polish it by hand on a polishing motor.

Jewellery tumbler (polisher).

Steam Cleaner

Not essential but a brilliant piece of equipment to remove all the dirt and grime from behind ring settings etc. It is just a large tank of distilled water that is heated up to boiling point. A foot pedal releases the steam under high pressure through a nozzle directed at the jewellery. Extreme care is needed when using this machine due to the heat of the steam.

Before putting the jewellery under the steam, always check for loose stones and if in doubt as to whether one may come loose, put the item in a mesh ball to catch anything that may dislodge. Use long rubber or plastic-tipped tweezers to hold the item to ensure your hands are kept well out of the way of the steam.

As with the ultrasonic, there are stones which you should not place under the steam; these can be found at the end of the book.

Draw Plate

Draw plates are rectangular steel plates with a variety of tapered holes in them. They are used for reducing the diameter of wire. This saves us having to keep a complete size range of wires in stock, which can be costly. You could splash out on a draw bench to hold the draw plate and to assist drawing down the wire, but you can also fasten the draw plate in your vice and simply pull your wire through.

SOLDERING TOOLS

There are lots of torches available but we do not need the biggest and best torch for repairing jewellery. In this chapter we will look at the options available and discuss the torches suitable for the repairs described in this book.

Portable Hand-Held Torches

Often referred to as crème brûlée torches or chef's torches, as they are used to add that crunchy topping to deserts. The small torch sits nicely in your hand and has the controls right at your fingertips to turn it on and off and adjust the flame. The gas that we use with these torches is butane, bought as disposable cigarette lighter fuel. This can be purchased at newsagents and DIY stores and is readily available in most towns.

Despite their small size, you will be amazed at what you can produce using these small torches. The flame size and

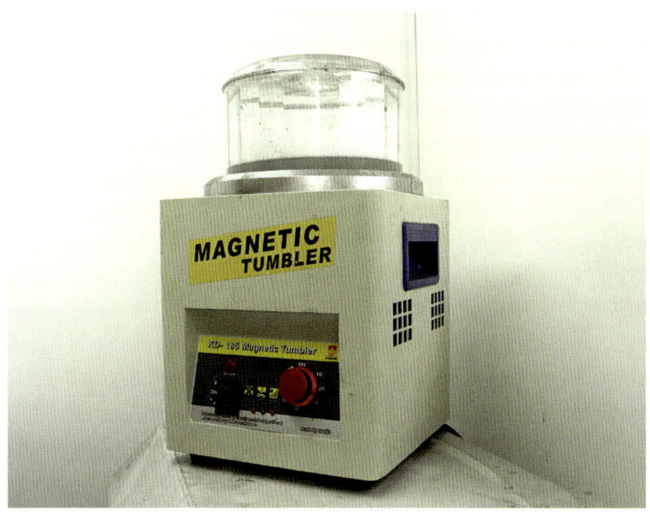

Magnetic polisher.

Steam cleaner.

Assorted draw plates.

therefore temperature is usually regulated via a small sleeve around the nozzle. When the sleeve is open, air is drawn through the nozzle by the gas and it is ignited by the electric trigger on the torch. If the sleeve is closed then less air is drawn in and the flame is not as hot, and is bushier. I always leave the sleeve on my torch fully open and simply control the heat of the flame by moving it near or further away from the piece that I am soldering. It's only when you start making larger pieces with bigger pieces of metal that you would need the larger hand-held torch. Sometimes you need a larger flame, as the smaller flame would not be able to cover a larger area without the piece cooling down before the solder flows.

The larger torch is just the big brother of the smaller torch. Usually everything about it is the same, it is just generally bigger overall which means it holds more butane and the flame is larger.

Bottled Gas Torches

I started out with one of these torches because we had them in university, and I didn't know about the small hand-held torches back then. You can buy the torch from jewellery tool suppliers and also plumber's suppliers. The handle is attached to a rubber hose that is connected via a regulator to a gas bottle, usually propane in the UK. Bottles of propane are available in several sizes and can be bought at gas suppliers, although you may have to travel some distance to get them as not every town has one. You can also purchase oxygen bottles at the gas suppliers if you use a dual gas torch such as an oxypropane or oxyacetylene torch (Smith's Little Torch).

The best part of these torches is that you can get interchangeable burners for them. You can buy a 'pencil' burner that provides a small, neat flame, similar to the small hand-held torch, but then you can change to bigger ones that produce a larger flame that is capable of melting large amounts of silver and gold.

Because of the extra components associated with this torch, there is more to check and observe. Make sure that all the connectors are secure and do not leak gas; the hose needs to be looked after too. These torches are not self-igniting so some means of lighting them is needed.

Soldering Surfaces

There are quite a few products available to use when soldering to protect your surface. Bricks and boards are inexpensive and will last you years, and just when you think it's time to buy a new one, they usually can be renewed and have a new lease of life. I use two types of soldering surface; one is a board and the other is a block. You can have a dedicated soldering area, or do as I do and have it on your workbench. You can technically do with just one of them, but I put the block on top of the larger board, as further protection against burning and damaging your surface. I don't tend to use kiln bricks as these absorb the heat and will certainly not help you solder efficiently. Whilst there are other types of soldering surfaces available, the following two are my most tried and trusted.

Soldering Boards

Boards are usually 6in or 150mm square and can be 6 or 9mm thick. They are made from a heat-resistant material that does not absorb the heat but reflects it back onto the item you are soldering. The board can be soldered upon directly or a soldering block can be placed upon the board. I have made a soldering station from four 300 × 300mm, 9mm-thick boards, which offers a lot of safety and surface protection.

Assorted torches – butane (hand-held) and oxypropane.

Soldering accessories – borax cone and brush, solder boards, solder pick and 3rd hand (cross locking tweezers).

This soldering area is made from four 30cm square, 9mm thick soldering boards.

Soldering Blocks

Blocks are usually 6 × 4 × 1in (150 × 100 × 25mm) and again are made from a heat-resistant material. My block gets the most wear and I have 'renewed' it several times by rubbing it on concrete to make the surface clean and smooth again. You can push pins or panel pins into the block to help hold your items whilst soldering, and even carve holes into it when you want to make completely round balls.

Fluxes

There are many fluxes available on the market. I have always used borax. It is available in a short cone and is rubbed onto an unglazed dish or tray with a little water to make it a runny 'cream like' consistency.

Borax – Available in a powder form or a solid cone shape. I always use the cone shape when soldering.

Borax Dish – A specially made dish or tray which is unglazed so the action of rubbing the cone onto the dish produces a powder that makes a creamy paste when mixed with a little water.

Liquid Flux – You can buy ready-made flux as a liquid but I find that you need to keep the bottle closed as it tends to evaporate. The shipping of this type of flux is expensive due to it being classed as a dangerous liquid, whereas borax is cheap to post as it is a natural substance.

Flux Brush – Any type of natural bristle brush is best. You can use a specially made borax brush or you could use a cheap artist's brush. The brush is used to apply the flux onto your join and also to transport your solder directly to where you need it to be.

Pickle

A strange word, I hear you say. Traditionally diluted sulphuric acid was used, but nowadays there are a few alternatives, some natural and a few chemical. You can use a dilute solution of citric acid or alum, or you can buy a safety pickle from your tool supplier. This is usually sodium bisulphate. I use it as a saturated solution, meaning I mix the dry granular powder into warm water with a wooden stick until no more powder dissolves. I keep the container warm in a baby bottle warmer or a commercially available pickle pot.

Heat Barrier or Heat Insulating Paste

We use either Thermo-Gel or Cool Heat. It is an insulating paste that keeps heat-sensitive areas of your workpiece cool when soldering. If you have heat sensitive stones in a ring when you are resizing it, apply the paste approximately 4-5mm over the area to be protected prior to the soldering. Providing the paste has not dried out during heating, it can be returned to the tub to be used again.

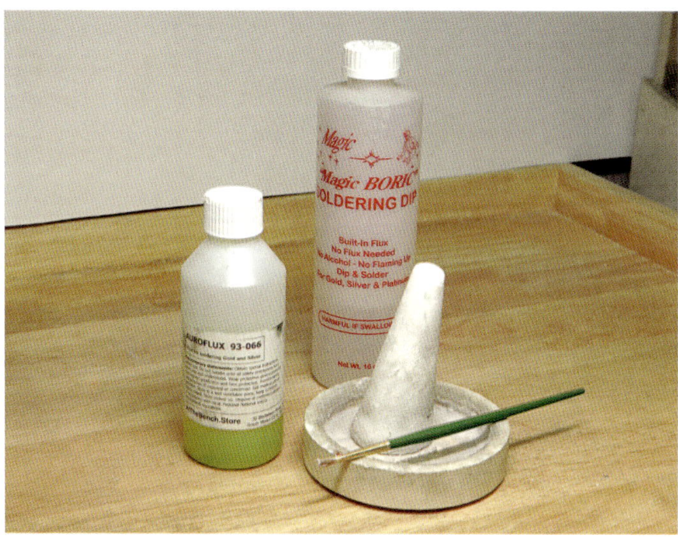

Flux – borax cone in dish (to be mixed with water), and pre mixed, ready to use.

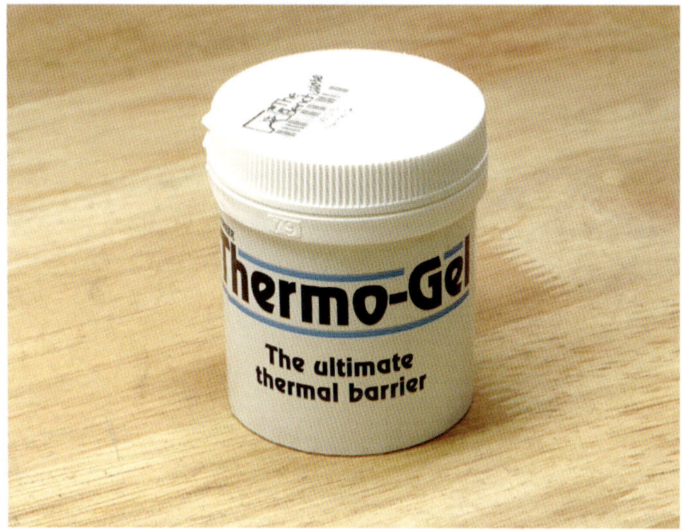

Thermo-Gel – heat barrier.

21 - mm
10 X

CHAPTER 2

MATERIALS

Let us take a look at what materials you need to keep in stock to be able to complete jewellery repairs. What you have to hand obviously depends on the repairs you carry out often. There is not much point holding onto a large stock of all the different sizes and carats of metal when you only need them a few times a year. You can order what you want from your supplier within a few days if you do not have it.

METALS

Round Wire

Firstly, we are going to be looking at what metal and also what section and size metal to keep on hand. Round wire is always a good shape to have in both silver and 9ct yellow gold. Any other carat and colour can be ordered as and when you need it. 1mm and 1.5mm diameter wire is the most common as these sizes can be used to make jump rings if you don't already have the size needed.

The wire can also be used to construct single ear wires for a client instead of having to sell your client a pair – unless obviously they've lost a pair. If you have a draw plate you can simply buy 1.5mm round wire knowing that you will be able to draw it down to whatever size you need for a particular job as and when you want it. This saves having to stock a lot of different sizes.

Square Wire

Just as a draw plate is useful for drawing down wire to the right size, having a rolling mill although expensive, is a necessity in the workshop because it can roll down wire or sheet to the exact size you need when you need it. If you don't have a rolling mill, it means that you will have to stock a few more sizes of metal, and your money will be tied up in material that you will not need as often.

2mm square wire is great to start with if you have a rolling mill, as from this square you are able to roll it down into D-section, rectangular section and small square section. If you do not have a rolling mill, it will mean that you will need to stock more sizes to suit the repairs you have in. I would have the 2mm square wire in silver, 9ct yellow gold, 9ct white gold and 18ct yellow gold.

Flat Sheet

Usually, you will not need to stock much sheet metal but if you have a resizing job requiring metal that is too large for your square or D-section metal then you can cut a piece from the sheet to the size required. You can carry stock of 2mm thick sheet, with larger pieces in silver than in gold due to the cost. Start off with 15mm square in silver and gold.

D-Section Wire

Most ring shanks are D-section or court-section so it pays to carry these shapes of wire. If you do not have a rolling mill then you will need a few different sizes: 2mm, 3mm and 4mm in width with the corresponding thickness would be appropriate both in silver and 9ct gold.

Most other sections of metal or sizes can be ordered from your bullion suppliers but hopefully the mentioned sections and sizes will cover most eventualities.

OPPOSITE: Gemstones.

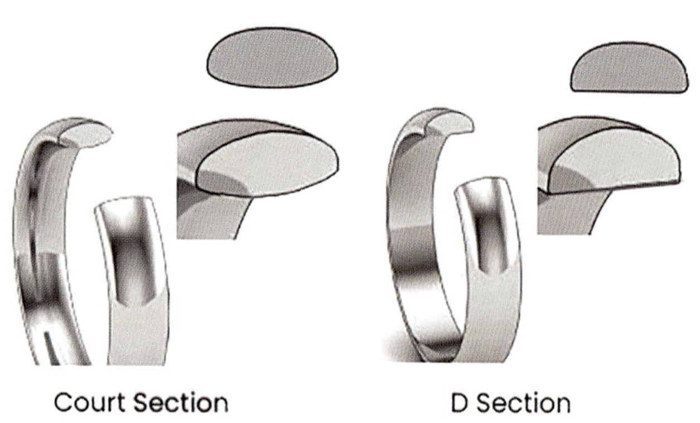

Ring sections.

FINDINGS

Findings is a term given to the clasps, ear wires, ear posts, safety chains, jump rings and so on that jewellers use to help them finish their creations. Whilst these items can be made by hand individually, it is often more economic to buy them ready made.

Jump Rings

These are small round rings made from round wire. They come in a variety of sizes from 2mm diameter right up to 10mm diameter in a light, medium and heavy weight, and are available in a variety of metals. Primarily you will be stocking silver and 9ct yellow gold jump rings in sizes 2mm, 3mm, 4mm, 5mm and 6mm in a medium and heavy weight. Anything over 6mm you can make yourself from wire or buy in when needed.

Ear Wires and Earring Posts

There are several styles of ear wires available. The selection in silver is greater than in gold, so it is natural to stock more in silver.

We stock silver and gold posts. There is usually one standard size of 0.8mm or 0.9mm thick wire and around 11mm long. If you need anything different you can make them up to order.

Bolt Rings

Bolt rings are available in a variety of sizes and metals and come in a light and heavy weight. We usually stock 5mm in

Assorted jump rings.

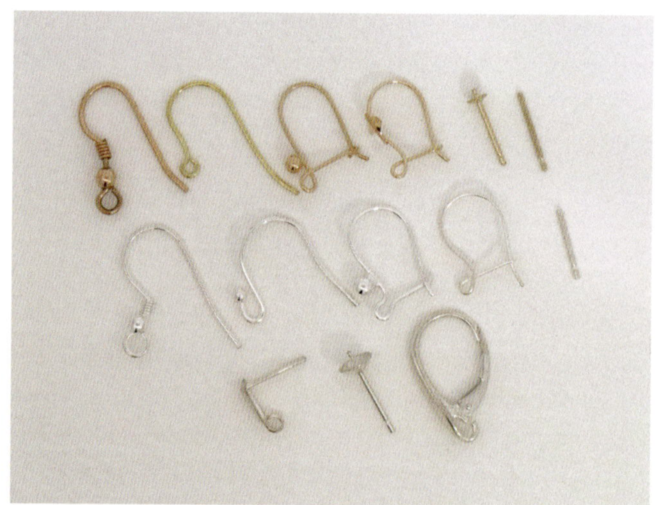

Assorted earring findings for drop and stud earrings.

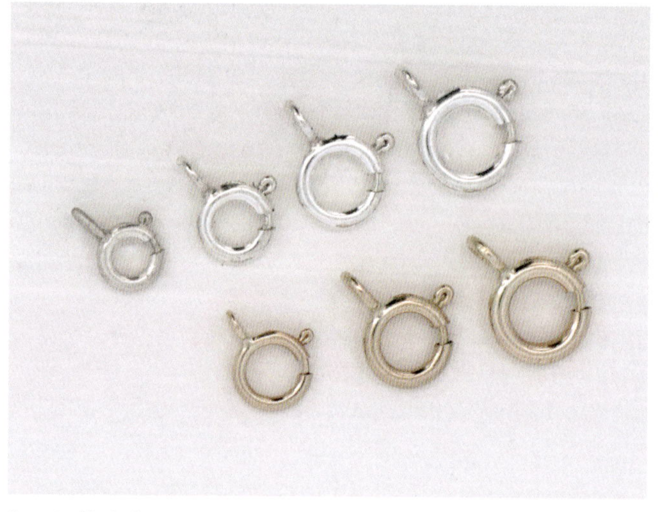

Assorted bolt rings.

a light weight, 6mm in a light and heavy weight and a few in 7mm light weight both in silver and 9ct gold.

Trigger/Lobster Clasps

This type of clasp is available in a few different designs. They all do the same job and no one design is better than the other, so you can keep a few of the different styles in stock to replace broken and worn-out clasps with one that is of a similar design. We stock more in silver than gold due to the cost, in 8mm, 9mm, 11mm and 13mm. Some come with attached jump rings, others don't.

Safety Chains

Available in bracelet, necklace and brooch styles, both silver and gold. We don't often fit brooch safety chains as brooches are out of fashion at the moment. Bracelet safety chains are available in light weight and heavy weight so we tend to stock both in 9ct yellow gold and in silver. Necklace safety chains are seldom used so we would order these in or just stock one silver and one gold.

Bails

Bails are attachments on pendants which enable them to hang from chains. A pendant hanging from a chain is going to wear through the bail before the chain wears through, so we need to keep a few bails in stock. Some people simply put jump rings through the pendant for it to hang on the chain and whilst there is nothing wrong with this, it does not look as good as a purpose made bail. It is usually a little more expensive than a jump ring but I would always offer the client a bail first and if that seems too expensive then a jump ring would be the next option.

Bails can be cast or they can be stamped out. Obviously cast bails are best but usually stamped bails are satisfactory. They have to be soldered to make them secure. We stock silver and 9ct gold stamped bails along with a few cast silver bails.

Chain Ends

These are shaped, folded pieces of metal that often go over the ends of heavier chains. Due to the weight of these chains, the chain ends wear out so it pays to keep a selection of 4mm, 5mm, 6mm, 7mm and 8mm in silver and gold.

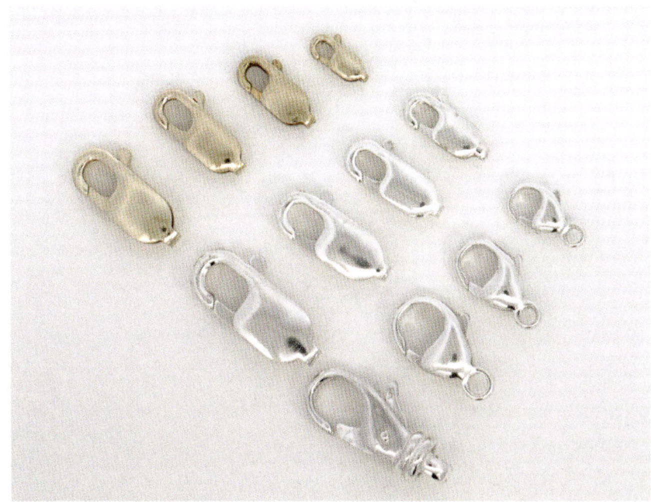

Assorted lobster clasps.

Assorted safety chains.

Assorted pendant bails.

Brooch Fittings

Brooches are not as popular as they used to be, but we still have them in to repair, so we keep a few hinges, revolver catches and pins in stock, mostly silver.

GEMSTONES

It is impossible to stock every gemstone that you're likely to come across whilst repairing jewellery, but it's worth stocking a small selection of typical stones in common sizes. Stones can easily be purchased from a stone merchant. When you require a particular stone that you don't have in stock or it's of an unusual colour or shape, you can send the whole item off to a stone merchant to match up a stone for you. Although they won't set the stone, it would be returned with the item so you can set it.

Cubic Zirconia

A lot of white stone dress rings made these days use Cubic Zirconia stones. They are relatively cheap and can be readily stocked. We stock 1mm, 1.25mm, 1.5mm, 1.75mm, 2mm, 2.25mm, 2.5mm and 3mm.

Diamonds

We have a selection in our safe but with so many clarities and colours available it is impossible to stock all the variations. We keep 0.9mm, 1mm, 1.25mm, 1.5mm, 1.75mm and 2mm in stock but only a few of each size. Clarity? We just ask our stone merchant for commercial quality which fulfils the majority of replacement diamonds. If you have the chance of buying any scrap or unwanted rings containing diamonds then remove these stones as they can often be reused.

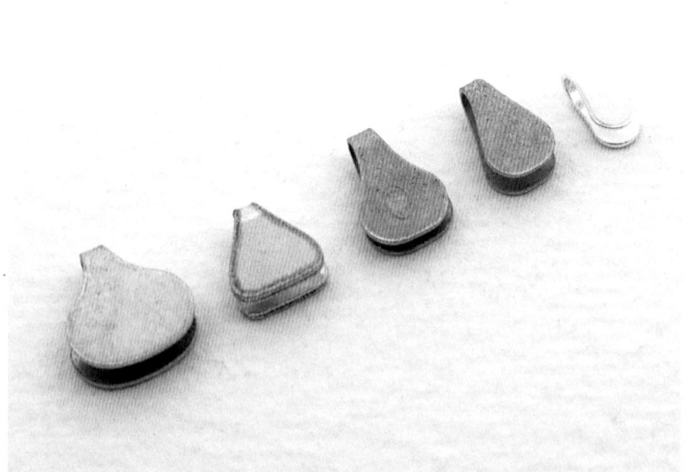

Assorted chain ends.

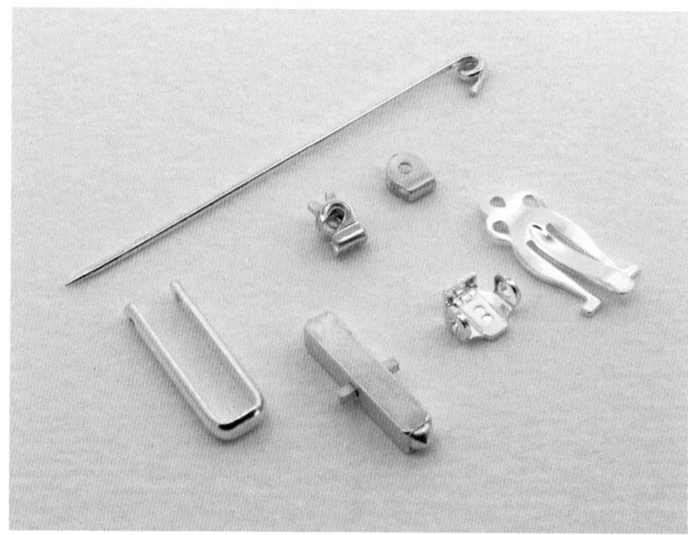

Assorted brooch and cufflink fittings.

Garnets

Not as popular these days, but a small selection will be advisable as they are inexpensive. 2mm, 2.25mm, 2.5mm, 2.75mm and 3mm are the ones to keep in stock.

Sapphires

The majority of sapphire you will be replacing will be the almost black sapphires with the slightest hint of blue. These are inexpensive but you have to be careful as these cheaper stones can be poorly cut. They may be deeper which makes them awkward to set, so be selective and try to get sapphires in a good cut with correct proportions. Sizes 1.5mm, 1.75mm, 2mm, 2.25mm and 2.5mm are the popular sizes.

Rubies

These can be expensive if you have the bright red colour, so it's wise not to stock up on too many rubies. Get some commercial quality and look out for deep-cut stones. Like sapphires, these will be difficult to set. Go for the slightly pinker stones in a few sizes: 1.5mm, 1.75mm and 2mm.

Chatons

These are glass with foil on the backs to mimic bright sparkly stones. These are often used in costume jewellery and watch bezels of the designer brand watches. You can buy an assortment of 144 that are all different sizes. They are usually cemented into place with a rubber cement called Hypo Cement. Do not use super glue as this dries white and will often cloud the chatons.

Marcasite

Again, these can be bought in bulk in an assortment of sizes. Marcasite jewellery has been really popular over the years and we often get rings and brooches in to replace the stones. They are simply cemented into place using Hypo Cement.

Assorted gemstones.

Marcasite.

CHAPTER 3

REPAIRING CHAINS

Whenever we take on new goldsmiths, the first job I get them to do is solder chains. I get an old silver chain that has large links. I cut one of the links and then get the goldsmith to solder it back. Then I break another and they solder that one and so on. Each time the goldsmith learns the way the link goes together, the amount of solder needed to make an invisible join and the amount of heat needed to make a satisfactory join. I then present the goldsmith a finer chain and we go through the whole process again. Boring as this may be, it serves a purpose. To refine the skill needed to solder the most delicate chains simply and efficiently.

Do not coat the area to be soldered with flux or another type of protective coating; this will only encourage solder to flow. Chains are usually made from solder-filled wire and if the solder on the adjacent links starts to melt, that flux will encourage the solder to flow and the links will be soldered together. Only apply flux to the break in the link that needs soldering. The discolouration on the metal from the heat of the flame will discourage the flow of solder on the other joins.

The amount of solder has to be as minimal as possible for several reasons. Too much solder will cause several links to be soldered solid and also there would be too much filing and polishing to be done, which is very difficult to do on fine chains. The size of the flame of the torch is important – often the actual flame doesn't even touch the chain link, which prevents discolouration of the link. The size of the flame is determined by the size and thickness of the link but on the finest chains the flame is brought down towards the join that has been positioned so that the join is at the top

and the rest of the chain dangling below. The join is close-fitting with a small amount of flux covering the join.

The smallest amount of solder is added on top of the join. As the flame is moved down towards the join, the heat that is given off by the flame starts to heat up the join and as the link and solder are very small it only takes a matter of seconds for them to heat up to the point where the solder starts to melt. You can control the speed at which the solder melts by moving the flame accordingly: away to slow things down, nearer to speed things up.

Once the join has been soldered, place the join in the safety pickle for a few moments to remove any flux and discolouration. You should try to avoid polishing chains on a large polishing motor as you run the risk of the chain catching in the mops. It could be sharply whipped from your hand and spun violently around usually catching your hand many times before you have the chance to move it out of the way. If you must use a rotary device then wrap the chain around a piece of wood and keep the chain tight around it. This way it is less likely to catch in the polishing mops.

SOLDER PASTE

I usually do not like to use any form of solder paste but when it comes to fine chains, the precise amount of solder and flux dispensed from the syringe can be located exactly where you need, and you won't have to worry about adding too much solder and risking it flowing onto the adjacent links. Solder paste contains its own flux, so there is no need to add any extra.

OPPOSITE: Chain being soldered.

Polishing by Hand

If you decide not to polish the chain with a bench-mounted polishing motor, lay it flat across your bench peg and hold it down taut with your fingers. Use your flex shaft with a bristle brush at a low to medium speed and gently polish the chain between your finger and thumb. Polishing the chain in this way, section by section, is a lot safer than using a large polishing motor.

SIMPLE LINK CHAINS

Repairing chains is a great way to start repairing jewellery, and a technique that can be practised on inexpensive silver chains. The idea is to use the smallest amount of solder to be able to make the repair as invisible as possible. If the client picks up the piece of jewellery that you've repaired and they cannot see where you have repaired it, then that is the sign of a good repair. It is a shame, but most of the repair work carried out literally goes unseen.

The first thing we have to carry out is an inspection of the chain. We must first look at the area that has been broken. Is the broken link still attached? If it is, can we reuse it? Take a look at the links adjacent to the broken area. Are they worn too? If there are too many worn links then it may be best to return it to the client undone, saying that a new chain would be better economically. Are they stretched out of shape? Can you reshape them? If they are stretched, this may be a sign that the chain has been pulled and there may be some other links that have fractured but not actually come apart yet. Take a look also at the clasp. Is that still working OK? All of this inspection should be carried out as part of the take-in procedure, as new clasps can be an upsell to the original repair.

If the old broken link is still present, then remove it and take a look at the links either side. If these are also broken or fractured remove them. You don't want to solder the chain only to find the next link along was also broken and you have to solder that one too. A simple observation could have saved you the time. If the chain is comprised of large links, removing several damaged links may not be possible, making the chain noticeably shorter. Contact the client and re-quote the job if that is the case.

You can use fine shears, flush cutters or a piercing saw to cut through the link. Decide on which side of the chain to cut through to rejoin it. If one side of the link looks a bit thin, then try to cut through this area. If not, look for the original join in the link when it was made and cut through that. No point in cutting through another part of the link only to find that when you try to solder your join, the original join opens up due to the heat and you end up with a link in two pieces.

Fracture in a simple chain.

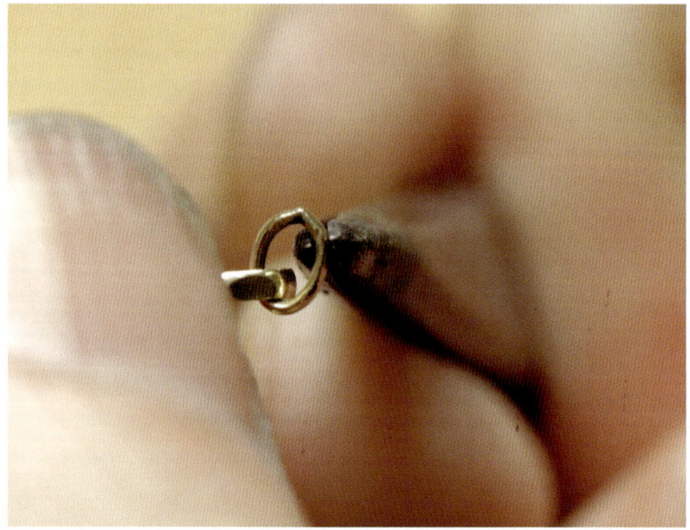

Inspecting the chain.

Opening the link with cutters.

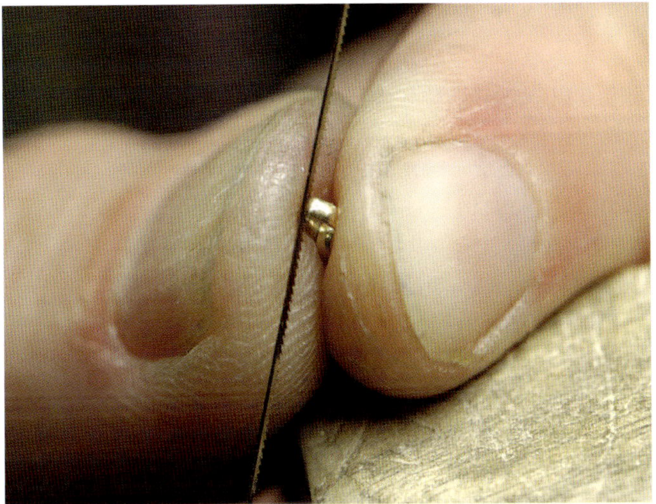

Opening the link using a saw.

Manipulating the link.

Cut through the link, and using a pair of tweezers to hold it, open the join up just enough to pass the other side of the chain through. You can do this with your fingers or use another pair of tweezers. Close up the link so the ends are touching. It is often easier to hold the link or the area behind the link with a pair of cross-lock tweezers. These can be rested on the solder block or they can be on a third hand base. Make sure the rest of the chain is hanging below or well out of the way of the join, as we don't want the other links heated up or accidentally soldered to the join.

If you use solder paste for soldering a link, of course the solder paste must match the same metal as the chain. An easy solder is best, as we will not have to heat the chain to the extent that other solder joins come apart.

If you are using wire or sheet solder, add the smallest amount of flux to the join followed by the smallest amount of solder. If your solder is thick, cutting a small piece off may be a problem. So pass the end of your solder through a rolling mill or hammer the end thin enough to be able to easily cut a tiny piece of solder.

With your piece of solder on the solder block, bring your torch towards it and just as it starts to melt, scoop it off the

LOCATING YOUR JOIN TO BE SOLDERED

If you decide to place the chain out flat on your soldering block, you can quickly lose the link you need to solder. Cut or scribe a faint line on your block and ensure that the link you need to solder is directly on that line. When you look away to get your flux and solder you will always know which link needs soldering.

Drawing a line on your solder block helps locate the link to be soldered.

Soldering the link closed.

Cleaning a chain – scratch brushing.

Polishing a chain – keeping taut to avoid injury, and damage to the chain.

block with the end of your tweezers or solder pick. Start to move the flame downwards towards the join. Often with fine chains the flame of your torch doesn't even need to touch the chain when soldering, as the heat from the side of the flame is enough to solder. Bring the solder onto the join with the flame on the solder. There should now be enough heat for the solder to melt and at the same time the join should be at the same temperature as the solder, and the solder will flow into the join.

Oxides usually occur on a chain when heated with a torch, but as we have used the side of the flame to heat the solder and the join, there should be hardly any oxides and virtually no clean up is needed. If there are oxides then you will need to pickle it until those oxides are removed from the surface.

The best way to clean a chain is to use a brass brush. Wrap the now soldered chain around your hand with the area that you have just soldered in the palm of your hand. Dip the brush into some warm water or hold it under a running tap, add a little hand soap to the brass brush and simply brush the chain with the brass brush making sure there is plenty of soap and water in the area you are brushing. This is effectively burnishing the metal. Although it will not give the chain a high reflective polish, it will make the chain lovely and bright.

Never hold chain in your hand and try to polish on a polishing motor! Using rotary tools can be very dangerous. You can buy what looks like a wooden bobbin, to wrap the chain around, and offer that up to the polishing mops,

making sure there are no loose ends of the chain dangling down. Any smooth cylindrical piece of wood would also suffice.

If you are very careful, you may be able to use your flex shaft to polish up small individual areas of a chain. Pull the chain across your peg and hold it firmly down with your fingers in an open manner and then lightly polish the section of chain in between your fingers. Keep the chain taut, otherwise the polishing mop may catch the chain and pull it away from you, spinning it round and round, damaging the chain. If you are not comfortable doing this, then scratch brushing it will be your best option.

Polishing a chain using a hand-held rotary tool – note that the chain is kept taut to avoid damage.

HOLLOW CHAINS

We frequently see hollow chains in the repair workshop. They are prone to breakage, due to the construction of the links. The links are made from hollow section metal to give the appearance of a thick chain, but the walls of the links wear away quickly due to the constant rubbing of the metal surfaces and the thinness of the metal walls. Hollow chains always cause us problems. If the chain has broken at one particular spot due to wear then it is obvious that the rest of the links must be worn the same way, so repairing one break may be a brief repair, as other links are likely to break in the near future.

Often the link will fracture, resulting in a staggered break, or sometimes a section of the link will break off. There is no way we would be able to repair this link, so it's best to remove it completely and work on the unbroken links. This may be a problem, as it will make the chain slightly shorter, and if the chain has a pattern of different sized links such as a figaro, then the pattern will not match. In this case you will have to decide what is the best option for your client. Make a solid replacement link to match the removed one, or simply resolder, resulting in an uneven link pattern?

The ends of the hollow link are going to be thin, so take care cleaning them up. Again, it may be better to remove the broken link if it is too weak and worn. To cut through the hollow links, take a look at the link and see if you can see the original manufacturer's join. If you can locate this then use your piercing saw to cut through this join. If you cannot see a join, cut through at the narrow part of the link so the join will be hidden under the adjoining link.

Be cautious as this can easily distort the link. Pushing the saw upwards with the teeth running against the metal is a gentler way to cut with less chance of distorting the link. If the link is small, then you can simply cut through with a pair of shears.

Carefully open the link by twisting it gently just like the way you open a jump ring. This will put less stress on the fragile link than if you simply pulled it apart. The ends of the link may have been squashed together and distorted if we've used a pair of shears to cut through the link. In this case slightly overlap the ends to create a larger area to solder. If the ends have been cut with a saw, then align the open ends flush with each other.

Hold the join in your tweezers and allow the chain to dangle down. Clasp the chain in your third hand just below the broken link. This way we do not put too much pressure on the hollow link to avoid it being crushed by the grip of the tweezers as it is soldered.

Make sure the join is perfect and flux it, being careful not to spread flux outside of the join itself. Direct your torch above the area we need to solder. Bring down the flame towards the join until the flux has dried and add your solder. Keep feathering the flame on and off to avoid over-heating the join and melting the link. Remember the metal may look thick but the walls of the chain are very thin and will easily melt. Feather the flame on and off until the solder melts. Look at the other side of the link to make sure the solder has flowed. If it has not, then add another piece of solder to that side to close the join.

What you have to remember is that solder likes to flow along surfaces with a greater surface area. It will not stay on the edge of the link but rather flow down it. You have

Fracture in a hollow chain.

Cutting open the link.

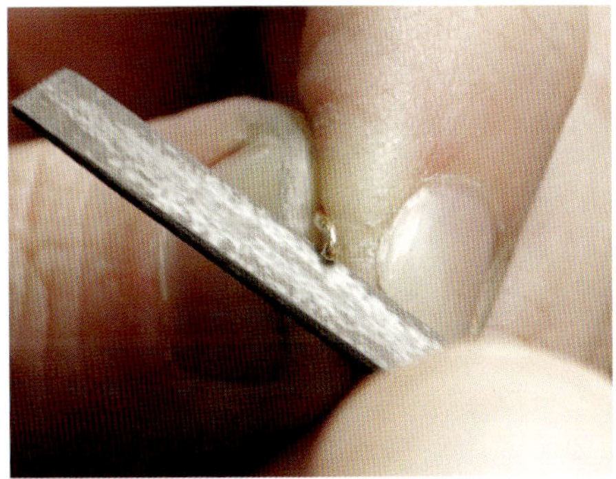

Aligning the ends.

to encourage that solder to stay on the end of the link by making sure that the two ends of the link come together evenly. Solder will always like to stay between two surfaces providing they are touching, similar to capillary action. This way the solder will stay between the join and not flow on the outside or inside of the link.

With this particular chain, it is too large to be able to scratch brush it; the links need cleaning up and polishing. It is too dangerous to do this with a polishing motor, so we opt for a fine silicone wheel and then a small calico mop mounted in a flex shaft or micromotor.

Soldering the link.

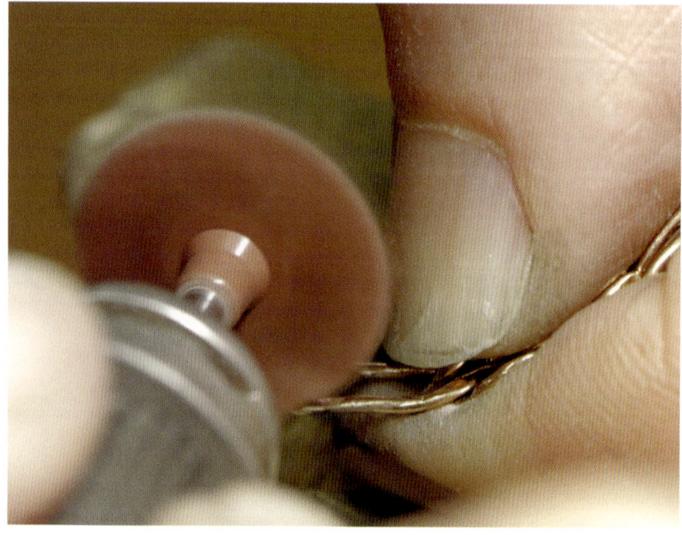

Cleaning up the area.

ROPE CHAINS

Rope chains are always popular, because being hollow they can be manufactured cost-effectively. As this complex type of chain is made by machine, it can cause us some problems when we come to repair it by hand. Solid rope chains are also available, which are less likely to break, however they cost a lot more when initially purchased due to the extra weight of the metal.

Before you start to work on rope chains, please make sure you clean the chain thoroughly, as dirt, creams and perfume get trapped between the links. If you use a torch to repair this type of chain all of the dirt will burn and become caked onto the gold, making it harder to clean it up afterwards.

There are two ways to repair a rope chain, one easy and the other more complicated.

Let's start off with the easiest
Using a pair of cutters, remove any broken sections on either side of the join. Cut back to complete round sections of links.

Take two jump rings of the same diameter as the chain and open them up. Link one jump ring through the second loop in from one end and through the first loop on the other and then close the jump ring.

Then take the second jump ring and thread it through the first loop on the first side through the first jump ring and then through the second loop on the other side and close it.

There should be no need to solder these jump rings (marked with black ink for you to see) as they are a lot stronger than the original hollow chain.

Now onto the harder method
Remove any broken sections at both ends of the break until you get to complete round links. Use a very fine pair of flush cutters or tin snips to cut through each end.

Open up each cut slightly and weave the cut ends together so one cut end goes through a complete round link on the other side and vice versa.

Add some flux to the joins of the cut link and complete link on both sides. Trap a small pallion of solder in this gap and one the other side. Alternatively use a paste solder like we have here.

Using a gentle heat warm up the area. Don't use too hot a flame as this is likely to melt the hollow links. Concentrate the soft flame on the area where the solder is, and wait until the solder flows on one side. Roll the chain to the other join and heat up that join until the solder melts. Pickle well.

Use a soft bristle brush just on the soldered area to clean the solder join, going over the area where the flame was.

Wash with warm soapy water and wrap the chain around your hand with the repaired area on the palm of your hand.

Use a brass scratch brush with warm soapy water to brush the area as well as the rest of the chain to polish it back up. Often these chains are gold plated when manufactured so you may need to quickly gold plate the whole chain to bring back the original colour. The soldering will burn off the gold plate in the area and it will look unsightly if left to the natural colour of the gold.

Fracture in a hollow rope chain.

Removing broken sections.

Link one jump ring through the second loop in from one end and through the first loop on the other and then close the jump ring.

Then take the second jump ring and thread it through the first loop on the first side and then through the second loop on the other side and close it.

There should be no need to solder these jump rings (marked with black ink for you to see) as they are a lot stronger than the original hollow chain.

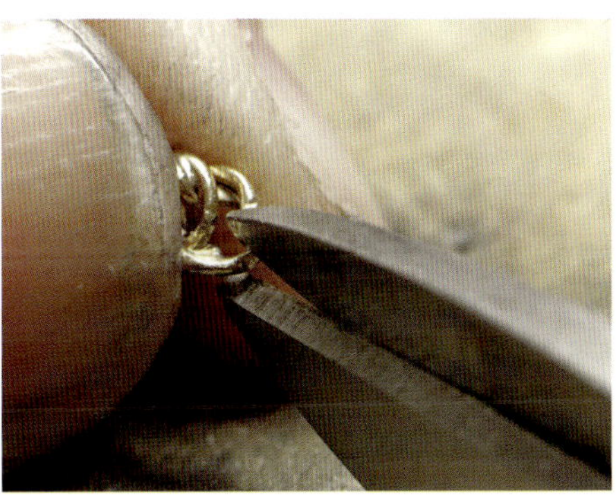

Removing broken sections.

Open up each cut slightly and weave the cut ends together so one cut end goes through a complete round link on the other side and vice versa.

Use traditional solder or solder paste.

Soldering the links closed.

REPLACING CHAIN ENDS

Chain ends are often used on medium to heavy weight chains. Due to the weight of these heavier chains, the chain ends wear over time despite their thickness. If we can catch the wear in time, we can often rebuild the ends with solder although this method is not the best as solder wears away faster that the parent metal. It is usually a cheaper and temporary fix until the chain end actually wears away. Depending on the chain end style we can often turn the broken ends together so they overlap and build them up with solder. Again, this is not the best type of repair, the correct way is to replace the old chain end with a new one.

Start off by measuring the width of the old chain end and source a replacement. You may have to replace both of the chain ends, which is usually a good idea because they tend to both wear out around the same time.

Paint some flux onto the old chain end as this will help the old solder flow and the ends will come off more easily. Position the end of the chain away from you in a third hand so the rest of the chain will not be in line with the flame. Heat up the chain end and pull off the broken pieces.

Prepare the new chain end by cleaning both of the inside surfaces with emery paper and then painting flux on the surfaces. Open out the ends a little to make the next stage a little easier.

Sweat-solder a small amount of solder onto the inside of each side of the chain end. This makes the whole process easier, as the solder is where it should be and it will not flow to the outside of the chain end – which might happen if we add the solder afterwards.

Clean the end of the chain, add flux and close the soldered chain end over the end of the chain, ensuring it is gripping the chain. Add some flux, position the chain as before with the end pointing away from you and warm up the chain end. The heat will be conducted onto the chain and when the temperature is right, the solder will flow onto the chain. You may need to turn over the chain and repeat the soldering to ensure the other side of the chain end is soldered. Applying a little pressure with your tweezers will help the chain end keep in contact with the chain.

Quench in pickle, emery the end using your buff sticks and polish. You can carefully use a polishing motor for this if you have one or you can use a polishing mop in a flex shaft or micromotor, taking into account previous advice.

Worn chain end.

Heating to remove old chain end.

Sweating solder onto new chain end.

Adding the chain end to the chain.

Applying light pressure with tweezers ensures everything stays in contact.

New chain end complete.

REBUILDING JUMP RINGS

Over the years if an item has been worn day in, day out, the small rings that hold pendants and catches will wear down due to constant movement in a small area. The wear can be consistent around the whole ring, if it is allowed to move, or if the ring is fixed, then the wear is isolated in just one place. If the wear is all around the jump ring, then it is best to simply replace it, but if it's in one area then we have a couple of options to repair it.

If a chain is attached to the bail or jump ring then it is best to remove it, as it is easier to rebuild the jump ring without the chain getting in the way.

The simplest way to rebuild a jump ring or bail is to cut through the worn area, file the link back to the original thickness and resolder it. This method works well if the link is large enough to function effectively after removing the section.

The other way we can repair it is to fill the worn area with solder.

With a small file, clean the area and then apply a small amount of flux just in the area that needs to be built up. If there is too much flux, the solder is likely to spread further than you want and you may end up soldering another part together by accident.

Use a pick to scoop up a small piece of solder matching the metal of the jump ring. Direct a small amount of heat to the fluxed area, and bring in the solder.

Continue heating up the jump ring. The small jump ring should heat up quite quickly and the solder will melt and flow into the worn area and fill it nicely, attracted by the flux and the heat of the torch. If the area still looks thin then you may have to add another small piece of solder so the area is the same thickness as the rest of the jump ring.

Pickle it, and then carefully emery the end ensuring the soldered area conforms with the rest of the jump ring.

If your solder has flowed and you have accidentally soldered another link on the one you were rebuilding, put your lit torch on its stand and hold the two items you have accidentally soldered together with two tweezers and bring the soldered area towards the flame. Put some tension on both pieces and as soon as the solder heats up and starts to melt, move both tweezers back and forth, take them out of the flame and keep them moving as the solder solidifies. This will ensure the two pieces will not be joined back together.

Pendant with worn jump ring.

Filing and fluxing the area.

Adding the solder.

Solder flows, filling the gap.

Buff with emery to smooth/finish, and polish.

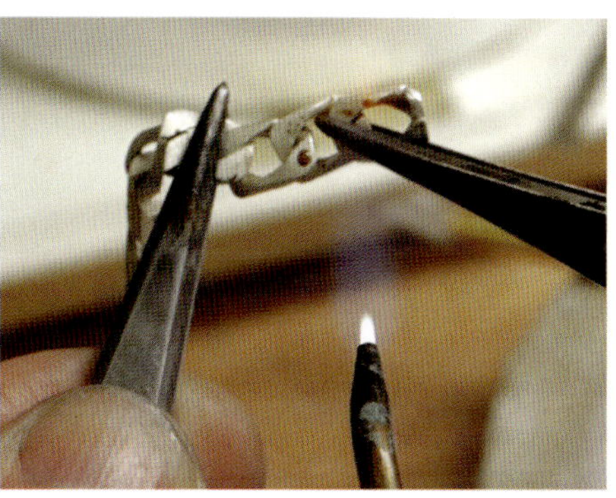
Reheating to release accidentally soldered links.

CHAPTER 4

RESIZING AND REPAIRING RINGS

Rings are one of the most repaired items of jewellery. Rings are usually worked to exact measurements to fit clients' fingers but fingers can get larger and smaller throughout life due to several factors, and it's our job as jewellers to make sure that they fit. Rings are usually given during memorable moments of a person's life, so preserving rings helps ensure that memories can live on.

A new ring must be made to fit the wearer. Throughout the years the ring will need to be made bigger or smaller for the wearer and if the ring is passed down a generation, then it may need to be resized again. Ring shanks wear out and need to be replaced. Claws wear down. Stones may have been lost. The ring may be totally beyond repair; if so the stones can be removed and the metal remodelled into something completely different, with the stones reset.

So you see, rings are one of the most important items brought to you for repair. The techniques needed to resize rings are basic, and ones that most bench jewellers will be able to carry out.

Locating Joins

There is one task we have to carry out before we even start to resize a ring. Firstly, we have to find out if the ring has a solder join already in the ring shank. This will help us decide how we proceed.

Take some tissue paper, wet it with plain water and then wrap it around the head of the ring if it is set with gemstones. Using tweezers, hold the ring by the wet tissue and warm up the back of the shank with your torch and as the metal starts to discolour; stop, remove the torch and examine the area to see if there is a join. As solder discolours in contrast with the parent metal you may see a lighter colour line in the shank. This will be a previous solder join.

If we are putting a piece into the ring, we would cut through that original join and add the extra metal. If there are a couple of solder joins already in the ring shank and we need to add another piece to make the ring larger then, ideally, we would need to remove the original piece in the ring and add a larger piece to the correct size. If we left the original piece in and added yet another piece, then there would be a chance that the original piece would fall out when we solder, making the job very difficult or weakening the ring by having so many pieces and solder joins. If there is no previous join then you are free to cut where you like, taking into consideration any special engraving or the placement of hallmarks inside the ring shank.

Also take a look inside the shank. Has the head and shank been hollowed out? How far does that hollowing extend around the shank? Ideally you should add and remove metal directly opposite the head of the ring. Any hallmark or markings should be off to one side of the shank leaving a blank area where we can cut through to reduce or add metal. Often, to reduce costs, the hollowing continues right around the inside of the shank leaving a small area where the hallmark or engraving is. This does cause us some trouble. If a hallmark is lost during a jewellery repair or modification, it is the responsibility of the person carrying out the repair to resubmit it for hallmarking.

Annealing Wedding Rings

When stretching or reducing plain wedding rings, it is essential to anneal the bands beforehand. New wedding

OPPOSITE: Soldering a ring shank.

rings have usually been die struck and fashioned into shape, and as such are work hardened. Annealing will make sizing these rings a lot easier, avoiding unnecessary stress to the ring, causing it to potentially crack or split.

Ring wrapped in wet tissue paper to protect gemstones from heat.

Checking the inside of a ring shank.

HOW MUCH IS ONE RING SIZE?

The measurement needed to remove or add one size to a ring is approximately:

UK, Australia and New Zealand – 1.5mm

USA and Canada – 2.5mm

Europe – 1.2mm

The actual size depends on the width and thickness of the ring shank.

Once you've acquired more experience in sizing rings, you'll be able to judge the exact amount to add or remove on a case-by-case basis.

REDUCING RINGS

Usually when a ring needs to be made smaller, a small piece of metal needs to be removed. If the ring is a plain band such as a wedding band of uniform thickness, then we are able to reduce it by shrinking it into shallow tapered dies. This technique works well on D-section or court-section metals that are not too wide. The ring is pushed and compressed retaining the original weight. This way is quicker that the traditional method of removing metal. If the ring is too wide then the compression will leave the inside of the ring slightly concave due to the conical dies used. Whilst this is not a problem, the outside shape of the ring also tends to distort, and may make the appearance unacceptable to the customer.

We will be using the lower part of the upright wedding ring stretcher for this job. It is comprised of a lever and a round disc with several tapered/conical holes in it. The round die is double sided with slightly different sized dies on the reverse. The tapered holes should be smooth to avoid marking the surface of the ring as it is compressed into the hole.

Firstly, make a note of the finger size on the repair packet.

Anneal the ring on your soldering surface, checking to see if there is already a join in the ring.

Then place the ring in the appropriate size tapered hole – 1 to 2mm of the ring should be above the level of the die. If the ring is level with the surface or is standing too proud of the surface then turn the die over and select the correct size hole on the other side.

Push the handle of the ring stretcher away from you to raise the plunger. Rotate the die so that the ring is beneath the plunger.

Pull on the handle to slightly compress the ring into the die. Push the handle away from you to raise the plunger and turn the ring over to compress the other side. Pull the handle and compress this side of the ring the same amount, pulling the handle towards you as far as you previously pulled it.

Remove the ring and check its size on your ring stick. Carry on this way until the ring is the correct size.

As the ring has been compressed the metal thickens up, so the inside of the ring may become slightly distorted.

Making a note of the initial size.

Anneal the ring and check for joins.

Positioning the ring in the reducer.

Compress both sides of the ring.

Check the size as you go along.

Buff the ring to restore the shine.

A quick file and buff will bring the metal back into a perfect finish.

If you are reducing flat section bands you will find that due to the compression of the outer edges, the inside of the ring will become slightly concave. This can be overcome by taking the ring down a little bit more than the size required and then putting the ring on the expanding stretcher part of the machine and stretching it up slightly to the correct size. This will help remove the concave outer edges of the ring. Only try this on narrow flat rings as the compression and enlarging may distort the outer surface.

You are able to compress rings with engraving or a diamond-cut pattern on the outside, too. When you place the ring into the die, line the hole with a soft cloth, such as a polishing cloth. We keep one on hand just for this purpose, as the process tends to cut holes out of the cloth. The cloth will protect the surface of the ring, so buffing and polishing will be kept to a minimum to preserve the detailed pattern. This technique is limited to the number of sizes a ring can be taken down – perhaps just one or two sizes smaller. Anything more than that would distort the pattern on the outside, so the ring would need to be resized by removing metal instead.

Compressing a patterned ring, with cloth to protect the design.

ADDING PIPS

Rings are one of the very few items of jewellery that are made to exact sizes to fit. As our bodies change over time, we may need rings adjusted accordingly. There comes a time when our finger joints become larger and the area between the knuckle and the finger joint may become thinner. When we resize the ring to fit over the finger joint it is just too large on the finger and swivels around. We need a way to prevent the ring turning when on the finger, but allow it to be big enough to slip over the enlarged or arthritic joint. This is where sizing pips are beneficial. It is a simple solution where we solder two small balls, or 'pips', inside the ring shank to take up the slack once the ring is on the finger. The ring can still be slid over the knuckle because the pips push into the fleshy part underneath the finger.

This technique is also used if the head of the ring is large and heavy, and tends to move around the finger when worn. The pips will gently press into the back of the finger thus stopping the twisting movement.

To start with, the ring needs to be sized to go over the enlarged knuckle. This can be achieved by stretching, or by putting a piece of metal into the ring band. Two small balls

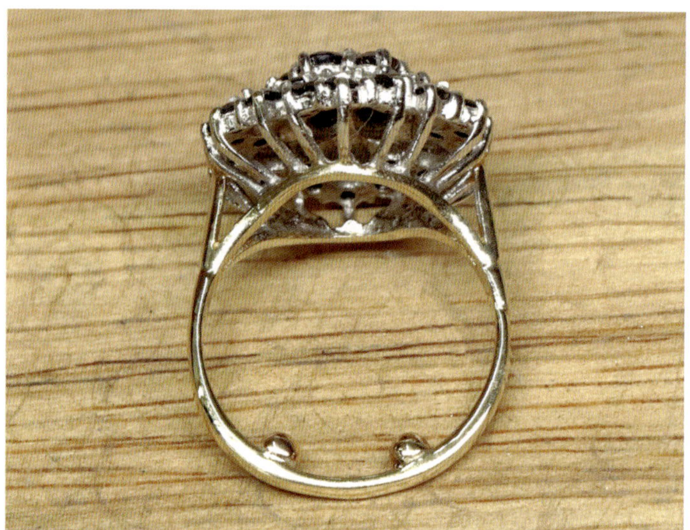

Sizing pips in place.

Making 2 × 2mm balls.

Marking the intended position of the balls.

Burring out depressions.

Sweating solder into the depressions.

Solder pips into place.

Using a white nylon brush to clean and polish the area.

corresponding to the metal of the ring are then made up by melting small pieces of metal on a soldering block. These are usually around 2mm in diameter.

Using a permanent marker, indicate where the pips are going to be soldered inside the ring. This is usually at the 5 o'clock and 7 o'clock position when looking at the side of the ring. These positions may not be possible if there are hallmarks or engraving in the way. You may have to change the pip positions to avoid these markings inside the shank.

A 2mm ball burr is used to make two slight depressions in the shank at the 5 and 7 o'clock positions.

Flux those depressions and sweat-solder some easy solder, matching the colour and carat of the ring, into the depressions. If you have filled the depression completely with the solder then use the 2mm ball burr just to remove some of the excess. We need a slight divot for our pip to sit into.

Clean up the pips and with the ring held in a third hand, position the ring so that the first depression is in the 6 o'clock position. Flux the area where we have sweat-soldered, flux the pip, and place it directly into the depression. Warm up the area so that as the solder melts, the pip sinks into the depression and becomes soldered into place. Repeat this with the other area we marked.

The shape and position of these beads should now match. All that's needed is to emery the pips and buff and polish the ring. A white nylon bristle brush is ideal for pre-polishing the inside of the ring shank and around the pips, as the bristles conform to the area being polished. If the pips are too large and the ring cannot be pushed over the finger, the height of the pips can be reduced a little to make it more comfortable.

You can hold the pips in place using another pair of cross-lock tweezers so that when you solder the pip it will not be inclined to move out of place. You must be careful here because the tweezers will absorb some of the heat from the torch, and there may be a temptation to overheat the area, causing the pips to melt.

CUTTING OUT GOLD

Check the ring on a ring sizer to make sure the size of the ring corresponds to the size written on the repair packet. Examine the area that you will be removing the metal from, to see if there are any previous joins. Sometimes you may see some excess solder, or the ring may be thinner in this area usually caused by excessive filing at the time of a previous repair.

If you cannot see any previous join then use the previously mentioned method: with wet tissue wrapped around any gemstones and held with tweezers, use the torch flame to gently warm up the bottom of the ring shank. As the heat discolours the metal, any previous solder join will appear as a faint line.

As we will be removing gold, it's always advisable to cut through any previous solder join so the shank doesn't end up with too many joins, causing weakness. For the inexperienced repairer, it is best to use a pair of dividers to mark out the amount of gold needed to be removed, starting off at any previous join. As you become more proficient you will be able to measure this by eye-marking off one size at a time.

Cutting out gold – start image.

Examining the ring.

Heating the shank to check for previous joins (with wet tissue to protect gemstones).

Measuring the amount to be removed.

Cut out the section required. Usually, when making jewellery, we like to cut on the waste side of our markings out, but when it comes to cutting out pieces for resizing it is always best to cut on the line. It is best to end up with a ring that needs to be tapped up very slightly after we have soldered it together. Clean up the ends of the shank with a fine file as often a slight burr of metal is left after cutting it.

Use a pair of half-round pliers to help ease the metal round. The area of metal for you to do this may be limited due to the size of the ring, or there may be stones in the shoulders. Areas where there are stones should never be bent or gripped by your pliers. Go easy on any areas that are hollowed out, easing the metal very slightly. It is better to have a slightly oval ring then a damaged one. Bring the ends of the shank together so they gently touch. The ends should be meeting flush with no gaps. If there is a gap then pass your saw blade through the join to remove any high spots. Once the ends are meeting nice and flush, flux the join all around. Capillary action should take the flux into the join.

Care should be taken if the ring has any type of gemstone in it. Certain gemstones are able to take heat, but it is always wise to protect them with Cool Heat or Thermo-Gel,

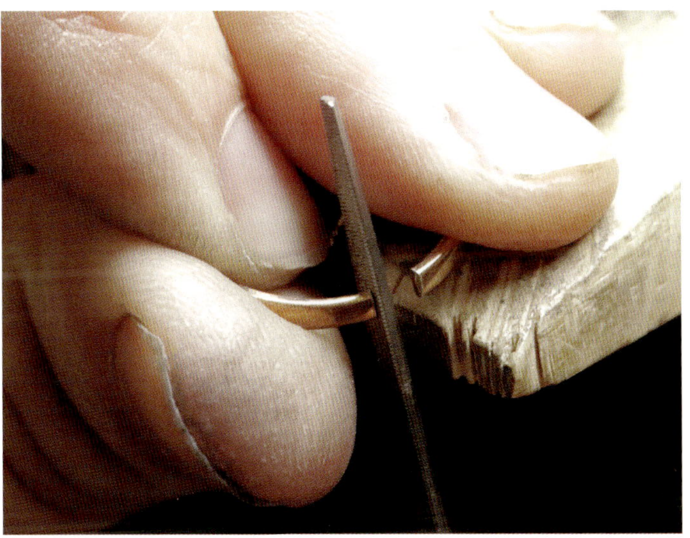

Filing the ends after cutting.

Easing the metal back around.

Ring is packed in Thermo-Gel to avoid damaging the stones.

Solder the joint.

Checking the ring size.

Straightening out the ring shank by tapping on steel block.

Finish and polish.

as these gemstones are your customer's, and will not be easily replaced should you be careless. Pack protection around the gemstones using the gel to stand the ring up.

Use a small pallion of solder of the same colour and carat as the ring. Always try to use a hard solder (high melting point) where possible, but if you are unsure whether there are any other solder joins near, then use an easy solder (a lower melting point solder).

Adjust the flame of your torch to match the thickness of the metal, i.e. a small flame for a thin shank and a larger one for a thick shank. Pick up the solder with a solder pick or tweezers and start to heat up the join, bringing in the solder. Heat the ring shank and not the solder as it is the heat of the metal that melts the solder and not the flame. This will make for a much stronger join. Once the solder melts ensure that it's flowed through the join by directing the flame on the other side of the shank to pull the solder through (solder always flows towards the hottest part and that is where the flame is).

Remove the gel and put it back into the container, and using a half-round file, remove any excess solder from inside of the ring. Then slide it on the mandrel to assess the size. If the ring is larger than the required size then you will have to resize it again. If the ring is a fraction small then it can be hammered up slightly using a rawhide or plastic mallet on the steel ring mandrel to the required size.

Tap the edge of the ring on a steel block to straighten out the ring shank.

Finish off the inside of the ring shank with a ring file, remove the solder and/or hammer marks from the sides and outside, and then start using your emery buff sticks to remove the hammer marks. A round buff stick is used to clean the file marks from the inside of the ring, or a sanding drum in a pendant motor.

Once you have gone down the grits of emery paper to around 800–1,000-grit, it's time to polish. We use two types of polish: a pre-polish and a high-finish polish. Pre-polish is the in-between stage, just after using the emery paper and before the final polish. Polish along the ring shank and try not to polish along the line of solder, as the mops can drag the solder and a slight line will show at the join.

Finish off with a soft woollen mop with some final polish. Use an ultrasonic bath to remove all the polish, and a steamer if you have one to blast any caught debris. Dry with a soft paper towel.

CUTTING OUT PLATINUM

Welding Platinum

People tend to shy away from resizing platinum as they think it's a difficult metal to work with. It is not difficult to work with; it is just different to work with. You should ideally have a few tools kept specifically for working with platinum – for instance, saws, files, emery boards and polishing wheels, as these tools can contaminate the platinum with the previous metals they were used on. Keep these items in a box labelled 'platinum', so no one can use them by accident.

You need to examine the ring to see if there are any previous joins. There may not be any if the ring is a wedding ring, but on a stone-set ring there may be some. This will help you decide which way is best to join the ring: to solder or weld. Welding takes a lot more heat and is only suitable if the ring doesn't have any previous solder joins in it. If you can see joins, then you'll have to decide if you can protect those joins from the heat involved with welding, as welding metal takes it above the melting point of the solder. We may be able to protect those past solder joins, enabling us to weld the join. Welding is preferable, as it is a stronger method of joining platinum than soldering, and it is invisible when done correctly.

Once you have determined how much metal you need to remove from the shank, cut out the correct size.

As we are going to fuse and weld the shank, it's best to use some of the piece we have cut out, as it is the same metal and the join will be invisible. Hammer or use a rolling mill to thin out the piece you have just cut out. This has to be made very thin, down to around 0.2mm thick.

Position the ends of the ring to meet perfectly, close and level all around.

Cut the section of platinum that you have just flattened to a piece 1mm bigger all around the section of the metal at the join. Put the ring on a tapered mandrel and pull it down until the join starts to open up, then insert the thin sliver and take the ring back off the mandrel, thus trapping the sliver in place. You will have to move it around slightly to ensure you have that 1mm of excess material extending all around.

There is no need to use flux on platinum as the metal does not oxidise, and if we did use flux, the temperature

Measuring out the sizes needed to be removed.

Cutting out the section of metal to make the ring smaller.

Hammering the small piece of platinum thinner.

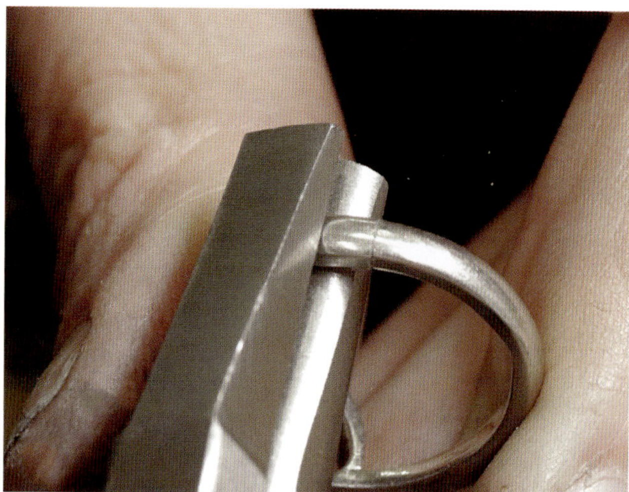

Bending the shank to close in the open ends.

Adding the hammered sliver of platinum between the join.

Always wear the appropriate glasses when welding platinum.

needed to weld is well above the operating temperature of the flux, so it would be burnt off.

The heat needed to melt platinum is also far greater than the temperature that hand-held single gas torches can reach. For working on platinum, we need to use dual gas such as propane and oxygen, or we could use a water torch. Both are easily capable of melting platinum.

We also need to consider the light given off by the platinum too. The extreme heat needed to weld causes the platinum to glow white hot and it is this light that is very harmful to your eyes. Plus, the light is so bright, you cannot see what is happening on your join. You need to use the correct eye protection. Do not even consider wearing sunglasses for this as they are not made to filter out the light rays. Spend the money on the correct glasses, as the light will damage your eyesight if you don't wear them.

Hold the ring in cross-lock tweezers if there are no stones in it. If there are any stones in it, use a thermal protection paste like Cool Heat or Thermo-Gel and add a nice thick layer over the stones. Platinum does not conduct the heat as much as silver or gold but we still need to take precautions. It is easier to protect gemstones than replace them.

Light your torch and adjust the flame to make it very hot. We cannot have a bushy flame as it will not be hot enough to melt the platinum. Put on your welding glasses and aim the hottest part of the flame at the extending sliver of platinum. Do not direct the flame towards the thermal paste. We need to melt this sliver of platinum onto the surface of the original metal for a successful weld to take place. You will have to move the flame around the ring to ensure that you can melt the sliver of platinum onto the ring.

Once you have gone around the ring and welded it, remove the heat and wait until the ring has cooled. You will find that the ring will cool down quickly compared to gold and silver, as it does not absorb a lot of heat. There is no need to pickle platinum as it does not oxidise.

File down the excess metal to conform to the shape of the ring shank. There are no short cuts when working with platinum. You need to work through the various grits of emery paper, getting finer and finer. This takes time to ensure all the previous marks are removed, working at right angles to the previous grit. Try to go to at least

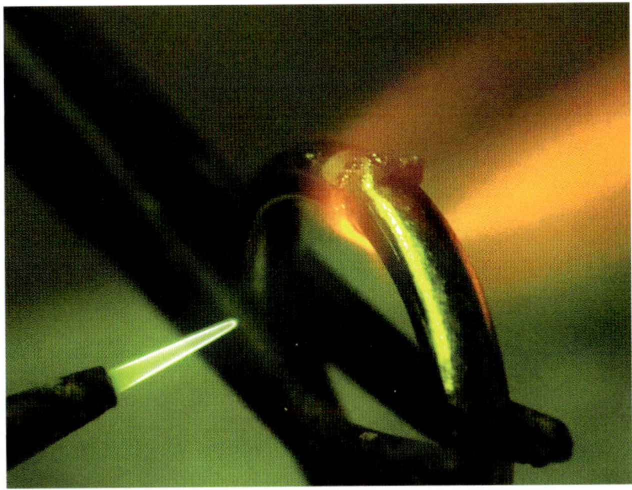

Welding the seam as seen through the platinum welding glasses.

The welded seam.

Filing the inside of the shank smooth.

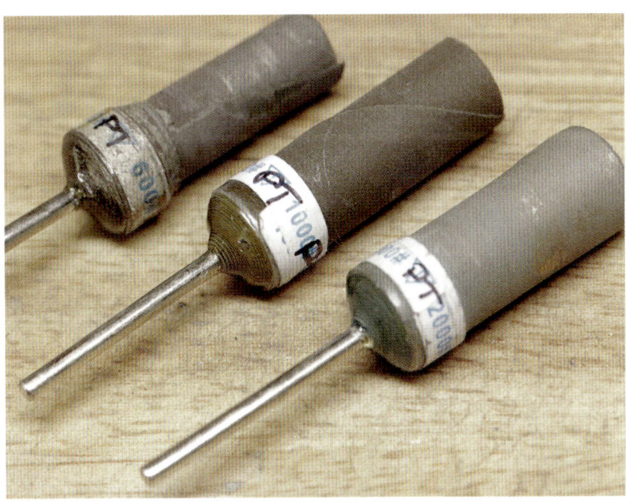

A selection of sanding rolls in various grits.

Using finer grit sanding drums.

Using finer grit buff sticks on the outside of the ring.

When hammering the sliver of platinum thin on a metal block, the piece may fly off the block if you do not hit it straight on. To avoid chasing it across the workshop, hold it down with a piece of masking tape.

Put some masking tape over the piece of platinum to stop it flying off the steel block.

1,500-grit so you don't have to spend a lot of time on the polishing wheel.

Use platinum-specific polishing compounds, as these are more abrasive than other compounds. Use a pre-polish then the final polish. You do not have to worry about solder lines showing as there is no solder – we have welded the join so there will be no telltale sign that there was ever a join in the ring.

Soldering Platinum

Welding is the best way to join platinum, but you can also solder. As with silver and gold you can get different grade (melting point) solders. And the best choice for a colour match is to use a solder with the most parent metal in, so the best solder to use is going to be hard or extra hard solder, called 1,700 as it melts at 1,700 degrees centigrade. This means that you will need a dual-gas torch, like the Smith's Little Torch to get the heat needed to melt the solder.

As with welding, platinum does not oxidise, and so you do not need to use flux either. You still need close-fitting joins that are perfectly parallel to each other and perfectly aligned – as you do when you are soldering other metals, so all the same principles apply.

When using solder, as you polish on the polishing mops, there is a chance that the solder will get dragged out (worn out), as the solder is going to be softer than the parent metal due to its alloy composition. Finishing off the join with progressively finer grits of emery is vital. Ideally you should need very little time on the mops to bring the platinum up to a shine. As there is a chance that the polishing mops could drag out the solder, polishing at right angles to the solder join is really important so the mop goes across the join as opposed to along it, wearing it away.

Take a look at the ring you are about to resize. Examine it with a loupe to see if you can see any previous joins. You will not be able to see welded joins but you may well be able to see previously soldered joins, either by a slightly different colour solder line or a slight line worn away across the shank. If you can see previous solder joins then use this as your first mark to measure from. What you do not want to do is measure either side of the previous join because the piece you cut out will have a join in it, and you will not be able to use the whole piece of platinum should you decide to add it to another ring shank to make it bigger in size.

Measure the number of sizes the ring has to be made to and cut through the previous solder join, if it has one. Make sure that the cuts are both parallel to each other.

Close up the join, bringing the cut faces together. If these faces are not parallel and not touching all of the surface then you can pass your saw through, taking off the high spots, bringing the faces closer together. If that did not bring the faces together enough, then saw through the join again.

Once you have the join meeting perfectly you are ready to solder. Due to platinum not oxidising, we do not need to use flux, we can simply cut a pallion of solder and place it on the join, or wedge between the faces of the join.

Using the platinum welding glasses, heat up the join until the solder melts onto the ends and make sure the solder has flowed all the way through the join. Finish off the ring in the same way you would if you had welded it.

Cutting through the platinum shank.

Inserting the platinum solder between the seam.

The soldered seam.

RESIZING RINGS LARGER

Hammering

When sizing up rings it is usually best to add metal to the shank, but often if the shank is thick and the size increase is only slight, then hammering larger is the quickest and cheaper option. This can only be carried out if the metal is thick enough and is in no danger of becoming thin.

Check the size of the ring and make sure it's the same on your ring stick as the repair packet states. If not, write down your sizes on the packet. This is why we always write the beginning size, the final size and how many sizes the ring needs to go to. Sometimes shop ring sticks are slightly different to workshop ring sticks, so even if the size difference is slight, the number of sizes bigger or smaller will be the same.

Look on the inside of the ring to see if there's any hollowing out, particularly on the shoulders. If there is, mark it on the outside with a Sharpie so you know to avoid that area when hammering.

As we are only hammering this ring half a size larger and not putting any heat on it, we don't need to clean it beforehand. Make sure the steel hammer face is polished and not marked. If there are any marks on the face, they will be transferred onto the surface of the metal and we will have to remove them when we come to clean up the ring later.

With the ring on a steel mandrel, using a polished-faced hammer, start to hammer. Use small light blows as opposed to hard heavy blows. Work around the back of the shank evenly, pulling the ring down on the mandrel as you go. Flip the ring over on the mandrel and continue hammering to even out the taper of the mandrel. Check the size of your ring stick and continue until the ring has gone up the correct number of sizes. When hammering, try to keep the profile of the metal the same; do not hammer directly on the back of the shank all the time, hammer the contour of the profile.

The inside of the ring will not need much cleaning up but there may be marks due to the hammering action forcing the metal into the line and size indicators on the ring stick. The outside will need a fine file to smooth out the surface. Start by hammering the sides on a steel block as the metal may have spread out slightly, resulting in a wavy shank. Next buff it with a buff stick.

Checking and recording the original size.

Tapping the shank evenly to stretch.

Finishing the ring.

Check hammer face for marks that could be transferred to the ring.

Filing and buffing the outside.

Next use a round buff stick or sanding drum on the inside. I often remove the outer edges of the inside of the ring to make it slightly easier to put on and take off. Use long, even strokes of the file on the outside, smoothing out the hammer marks removing as little of the metal as possible. Finish off with a flat buff stick, working down the grades, then polish the inside and outside. Polish the inside with a finger mop on a bench-mounted polishing motor, or white nylon brushes and pre-polish, followed by a large calico mop on the polishing motor and a soft mop with a final polish inside and outside the ring.

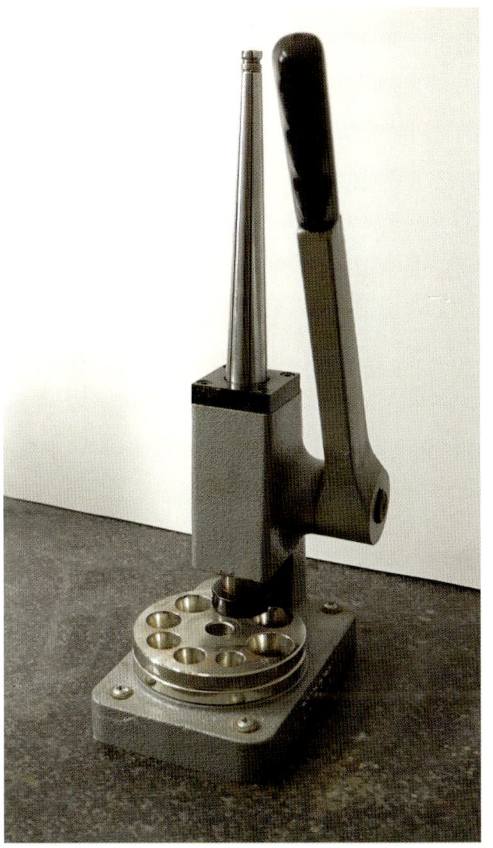
Upright
ring stretcher.

Stretching on an Upright Ring Stretcher

The quickest way to stretch a plain ring such as a wedding band is to use a piece of equipment called an upright wedding ring stretcher. There are a few models to choose from but fundamentally, they all do the same thing.

Depending on the construction of the ring, for example seamless with no solder join, the ring can be stretched up a number of sizes with frequent annealing to ensure the ring does not crack. If there is a solder join in the ring, then extra care must be taken, and the ring may only be able to be stretched a size or two without the join splitting.

What you have to bear in mind is that stretching the ring makes the metal thinner. Stretching the ring too much may be uncomfortable to wear. You will have to assess the thickness of the ring before you start, to ensure that stretching it will not affect the ring's integrity. Over-stretching could make the edges of the ring sharp and may cut into your client's finger.

A wedding ring stretcher is a round tapered mandrel that is split vertically into four or six sections. As the handle

of the stretcher is pushed away, the split mandrel is forced open, thus stretching the wedding ring that is placed over it.

The split tapered mandrel often has ring sizes engraved into the surface but these should not be relied upon. Instead, check on your ring stick to note the correct size. First, measure the ring to confirm its original size and check this against the size written on the take-in packet. Note any discrepancy.

Warm up the ring slowly with your torch until the metal starts to discolour and oxidise. Quench the ring in water, *not pickle*, to cool it down and then check to see if there is a solder seam in it. The solder seam will show up as a lighter colour against the oxidised metal.

Check and record ring size.

Heat up the ring and check for solder joints.

Anneal.

Ring on upright ring stretcher

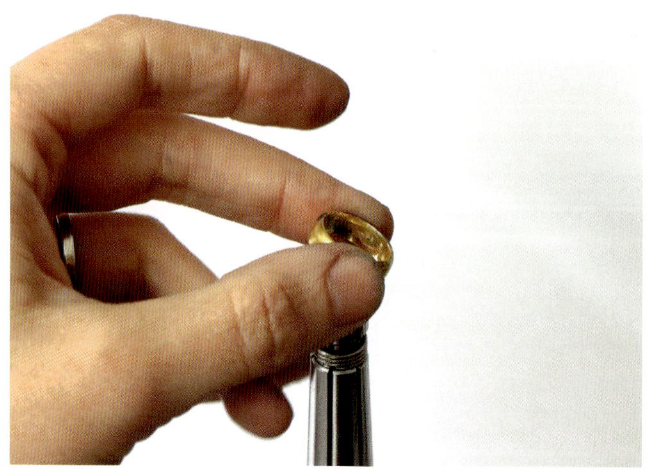
Ring is inverted and stretched again.

Anneal the ring evenly on a soldering block to a very dull red colour. Quench and then pickle the ring to remove any oxides.

If you cannot see a solder seam
Make sure the handle of the upright ring stretcher is pulled towards you, slip the ring over the tapered split mandrel down as far as it will go. Gently push the handle away from you.

As you do, the splines of the mandrel open out and stretch the ring. Don't push too hard in one go. Stop, pull the handle back towards you. Rotate the ring around the split mandrel 1/8th of a turn then gently ease the handle away from you again. Pull the handle back towards you, flip the ring over so the other edge is stretched evenly. Failure to turn the ring around will result in a tapered shape, which will be more evident on a wider ring. Push the handle away the same amount as before, rotate 1/8th of a turn, push the handle away. Remove the ring and check the size on your ring stick.

If the ring has a join in it
Bear in mind there may be more than one join. This may cause problems with stretching as multiple joins make the ring weaker. Take extra care when stretching; having the join positioned facing towards you helps, so you can keep an eye on it. If a ring is going to snap, it will snap right on the soldered join.

You may find that the ring stretches a bit more at this join, or the metal may be slightly thinner where the ring was soldered and previously finished. The join may also start to split due to a poor solder join. In any case, stop immediately and reassess how the ring is going to be resized. You could hammer it bigger, keeping away from the join, or put a piece in to the ring to avoid stretching it.

Once you have checked the ring on your ring stick you will be able to assess the force required to make the ring the size you need. To make the ring larger still, repeat the sizing operation. If you only need to take the ring up a fraction of a size more, then use less force when pushing the handle away from you.

Check the ring on the ring stick, making sure that you turn the ring over to make sure both edges of the ring read the same size.

Buffing the ring.

Polishing the ring.

There should not be too much cleaning up to do. The surface may look a little like orange peel due to it being stretched. This can be resolved with a buff stick, inside and out, and a polish using a felt mop or white nylon brush. A final polish on a soft woollen mop is all that should be needed to clean up the ring to showroom condition.

Using a Gem Ring Stretcher

A gem ring stretcher is a fantastic addition to the jewellery repair workshop. It does exactly as it is named: it stretches

If you have some engraving on the inside of the ring you can protect this by wrapping the area of the split mandrel where the ring is being stretched with some paper or a smooth cloth. This should stop any of the engravings on the split mandrel being transferred onto the inside of the ring when being stretched and the engraving being subsequently worn away when you come to buff and polish the inside of the ring.

Protecting engraving inside the shank when stretching a ring.

rings that are gem-set. It does this by rolling a small, grooved roller around the outside of the shank, compressing it and stretching the metal. It is a process that requires no heat and a minimal amount of cleaning up. It consists of a small stand that is screwed to the work surface. A handle is attached to a central pivot over which you place the ring. A box of rollers of assorted shapes and widths of grooves accommodates the different section ring shanks, so we are able to keep the same profile as we stretch up the ring.

A roller with the same profile groove as the outside of the ring shank is chosen. This is inserted into the handle and the handle tightened up, so that the roller is in contact with the ring. A little more pressure is applied and the handle rotated around the pivot point, turning the roller around the area of the ring shank, thus stretching it. The harder you apply pressure the more the ring will be stretched. It is advisable to frequently remove the ring to

Ring with hollowed out shank, and stones in shoulder.

Ring marked up where hollowing starts.

Selecting a roller for gem ring stretcher.

check its progress on a ring stick as it is easy to over stretch and thin out the ring shank unnecessarily.

The problem always lies in the fact that it stretches the metal, thinning out the ring shank, which is not always the best way to increase the size of gem-set rings. Starting with a thin shank and then using the gem ring stretcher will thin out the shank even more. Your client may well be unhappy ending up with a shank that is noticeably thinner than when they first brought it to you.

So, when do we use this type of stretcher? When the ring shank is thick enough to take a little bit of stretching, and then only taking the ring up one or two sizes. Anything more than that will make the ring shank noticeably thinner and that is not what we want.

This type of ring stretcher must be used with caution, as it can cause a lot of damage to the ring. Firstly, we need to take a look at the style of gem-set ring. Are the stones contained within a setting at the top? Are there stones in the shoulders? Are the shoulders hollowed out?

If there are stones in the shoulders then obviously, we cannot apply the roller anywhere near these areas or they will be flattened. If the inside of the shoulders are hollowed out, use a Sharpie marker on the outside showing where the hollowing out starts. You do not want to apply the roller over these hollow areas as the metal will simply collapse and you will have a really awkward time trying to reshape those shoulders. If the hallmark or markings on the inside of the shank are very light with not much depth to them then rolling over those areas will also flatten and push out the hallmarks or markings.

Let us see a typical example and show you how we approach stretching it on a gem ring stretcher. First of all, select a roller that has the same profile as the ring shank, to retain the ring shank section after we have rolled it.

Place the ring over the fixed roller and tighten the rotating roller towards the ring shank. Stop when in contact. Pay attention to any areas you do not want to roll.

Tighten the handle about a 1/16th of a turn with the rotating roller at the very bottom of the ring.

Move the handle to rotate the roller around the shank. You may be limited with this movement as you do not want to roll past any hollow areas you have marked. First roll one direction and then back the same amount in the opposite direction.

Loosen the handle and remove the ring. Turn the ring over and then tighten the handle until it just touches the shank. Tighten the handle that 1/16th of a turn and repeat the process, turning the handle one way and then back the other. We turn the ring over to compensate for any discrepancy in the equipment, ensuring we stretch the shank evenly on both edges.

Take the ring off and check the size on your ring stick. Repeat the above process if you need to go any larger, taking into consideration how much larger we made the ring with that 1/16th of a turn on the handle. Same again to stretch the same amount, or turn the handle a little less if required. I would not try to turn the handle any more than 1/16th of a turn, as this may make the ring too large, thinning out the shank considerably. You would then have to remove a piece from the shank to make it the correct size.

Once you have the ring the correct size, you will find there will be a gentle step where the original shank meets the area we have just stretched.

Use a file to smooth off this step and blend the two areas into a gradual profile. You may also need to hammer the edge of the shank if, when stretching, the back of the ring has stretched unevenly and the shank is wavy. Put the back of the ring on a steel block and tap the edge with a steel hammer being careful not to hammer any of those hollow areas you have carefully avoided when rolling the shank.

Go over the edge of the shank with a file. You may find the width of the shank has spread slightly so just file this back to how it was originally and then using your buff sticks to smooth away those file marks.

Then it is onto the pre-polish with a hard calico or felt mop. I love to use white nylon brushes for the inside of ring shanks with a pre-polish like tripoli. Ultrasonic the ring to clean off the pre-polish. Make sure any stones do not fall out of the ring. Putting the ring in a plastic tea strainer helps contain any stones that may fall out.

Dry the ring and then use a nice soft woollen mop with a final polish for the inside and outside of the ring. Pay attention not to over-polish the head of the ring that may contain stones, as we do not want to dislodge or wear away any claws.

Assembling the equipment.

Tightening the handle to secure.

Rotate the roller around the shank.

A gentle step indicating where the ring has been rolled – this will need to be removed.

Tapping the shank on a steel block to eliminate any wavy areas.

Filing.

Finishing.

ADDING GOLD

The first thing we do when sizing any ring is to look for any previous solder joins. Clean the ring in an ultrasonic bath first, and check the back of the shank with a loupe to see if a previous join is visible. If you cannot see a join, warm up the back of the ring shank slightly to discolour it, to see if any previous solder seams become visible. Solder will oxidise a different colour so the seam will show up as a lighter colour metal.

If there is any sign of a previous repair where gold has already been added to the ring then we will have to take that piece out. The piece of gold we will have to add will now have to include that section we have just cut out. We do this because we have to limit the number of solder joins in the ring shank. If we left that piece in the ring shank and then added the new piece, there would be an extra join in the shank and there could be a problem with the old piece popping out when we solder the new piece in place.

Cutting through the previous solder join will help remove the old solder. Use a parallel-sided needle file to remove any burr that may have been produced when sawing. Slide the ring up the mandrel to the size needed and measure the gap between the ends of the shank. This is the amount of metal needed.

It is always best to use sizing metal that is just slightly wider and thicker than the actual ring shank so when the

Heating the shank to check for previous solder joints.

Ring shank showing previous piece added.

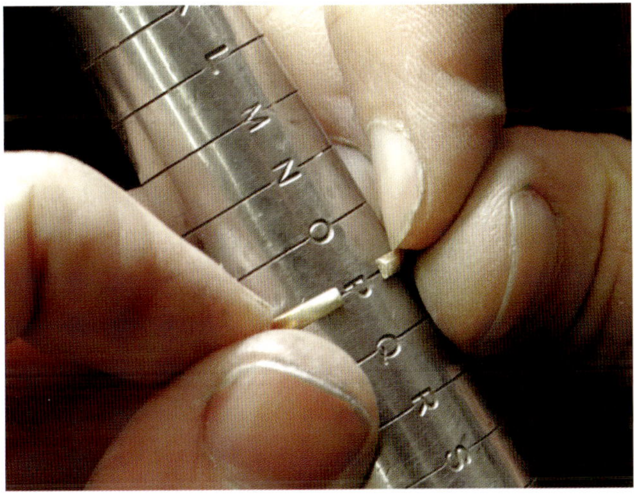

Measure the gap with the ring at the correct increment on the mandrel.

Putting a gentle curve on the piece to be added, using shank bender.

Measuring the sizing stock.

Positioning the piece.

piece has been soldered into place, we can blend the new metal to the same dimensions as the original ring shank. You can use a pair of half-round pliers to do this or a shank bender which makes the task a little easier for us.

Offer the sizing stock up to the gap in the ring shank and scribe it. Saw directly on the line you have marked. It is better to make the ring ever so slightly smaller knowing that we can tap it that little bit to ensure the ring is rounded.

With the piece of sizing stock cut, open up the ring shank and position the piece in between the ends. Make sure that the joins are nice and close, remove the ring from the mandrel trapping the sizing stock in place. It is best to position the sizing stock so the piece lines up flush with the inside of the ring shank as it is easier to remove the excess metal on the outside of the ring than the inside.

If the ring has stones in it, use heat protection paste around the stones to make a layer of at least 5mm over the

Thermo-Gel holding the ring in place, while protecting gemstones from the heat.

Holding the ring with head and shank tweezers, if it has no stones.

Soldering the piece into place.

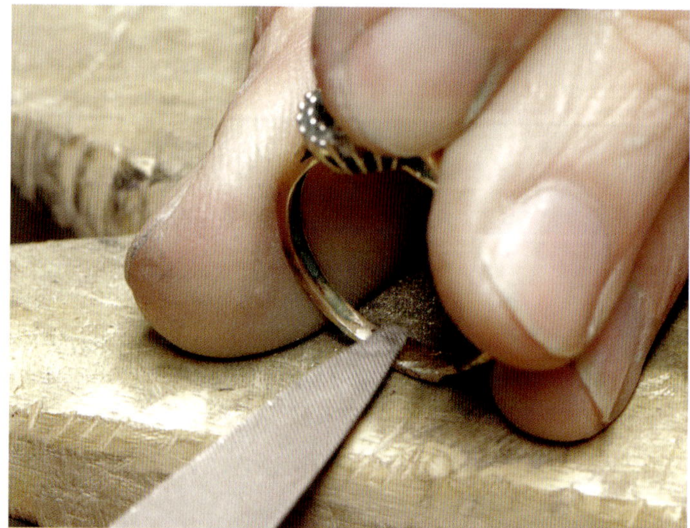

Filing the insert, removing excess metal.

stones. You can use this to position the ring upside down on your soldering block.

Alternatively, you can use a pair of head and shank tweezers to hold the sizing stock in place. This technique works well if the ring has no stones in it.

Flux the join. Cut two small pallions of easy solder matching the quality/carat and colour of the metal and place above each join. Light up your torch and adjust the flame according to the size and thickness of the shank. Gently warm up the area to make sure the flux does not bubble up too much and dislodge the solder. Start to direct the heat on the joins, moving the torch towards the inside of the ring. We are relying of the heat of the metal to melt the solder as the solder is in contact with the metal. The solder needs to be the same temperature as the metal it is in contact with. The solder likes to flow towards the hottest part so it is natural that when the solder starts to flow

Buffing the ring.

it moves through the join from the outside of the shank towards the inside, where the flame is, the hottest area.

If heat protection is used then wait for the ring to cool down before using the back of your tweezers to remove the heat paste and put it back into its container. Swill the ring in water and use a tissue to remove the rest of the paste. If there are no stones in the ring, then you are OK to quench it in the safety pickle. Rinse in water and dry.

Now it is time to start to finish the ring. Use a file to bring the sizing stock down to the same dimensions as the existing ring shank, making sure the outside profile is matched.

Now slide the ring onto the mandrel and gently tap it with a rawhide or rubber mallet to round off the ring and to check the final size. It is usual for the ring to be ever so slightly smaller, so start to tap the ring onto the mandrel with the mallet until the ring is the right size. Flip the ring over and make sure it is the correct size on that side of the ring, due to the taper of the ring mandrel.

Try not to remove any of the original shank as we do not want to make it any thinner. Switch over to your buff sticks to smooth out the inside and outside.

Next go over with pre-polish. You may want to polish the rest of the ring shank to remove any old scratches and marks to blend in the new piece you have just put in. A few moments in the ultrasonic and a soft mop with your final polish will bring back the original showroom shine. I would carefully go over the head of the ring, bringing back the high polish. If there are stones in the head then care must be taken around the claws not to loosen them or catch them in the polishing mops.

A final few minutes in the ultrasonic to remove the polish and then a quick blast with the steamer if you have one is all that is now needed, being mindful of any stones in the ring.

ADDING PLATINUM

Platinum can be stretched, but when the shank is too thin to do so or the client has requested adding metal, adding a piece of platinum is basically the same technique as adding gold. We can solder or weld platinum – welding is preferable – but when we have to add metal, soldering is a better option. Establish the size the ring is now, and the size it has to go to. Check those details are correct on the repair packet.

Platinum solder is available in various grades (melting points). Try to use the highest melting point solder, as with other metals, the solder with the highest melting point has less alloy in it so the colour and wearability is going to be more in keeping with the parent metal. This is very important with platinum, due to the way we have to polish it. We do not use anything less than 1,700-grade platinum solder.

Trying to find if there are any previous solder joins in the ring is going to be difficult with platinum as the metal does not oxidise when gently heated as gold and silver do. Examine the back of the shank closely. You may be able to see a slight line running across the shank, either on the outside or inside, indicating a solder join. If you can see a join then cut straight through it. If there is no join then take a look on the inside of the ring shank to assess the best place to cut, keeping away from any hallmarks and any hollowed-out areas.

Once cut open, gently slide it up on the tapered mandrel. If the ring has stones in it, keep an eye on the setting as you slide the ring larger on the mandrel to ensure it doesn't deform, and also do this over a workbench or your apron, just in case any stones pop out due to the tension being placed upon them.

Once the ring is open to the right size, take a piece of sizing stock that is marginally larger than the metal section you have cut through. Using either your half-round pliers or a shank bender, ease the metal into a gentle curve, matching the curvature of the ring at its opened position.

Make sure the one end is nice and square, rest it on the mandrel next to the gap, and mark off the measurements.

Cut the sizing stock on the line but to the waste side and clean up the end to remove any slight burr that may be left from sawing. Ensure that this end is also square. Offer up the sizing stock to the gap; you may need to slide the ring up a fraction larger to slip the piece in.

Locating any previous join.

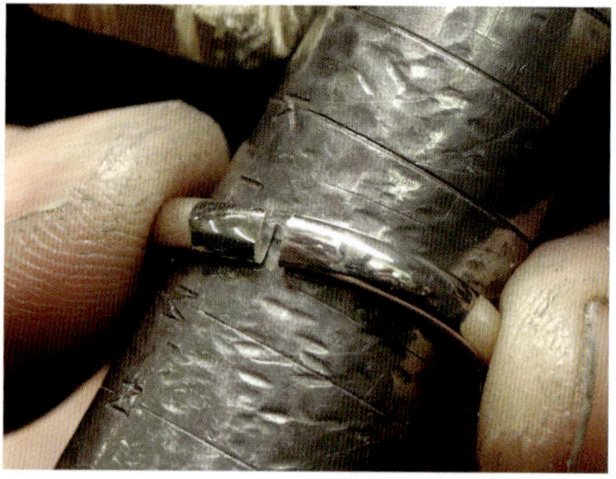

Gently sliding up the mandrel to meet the desired size.

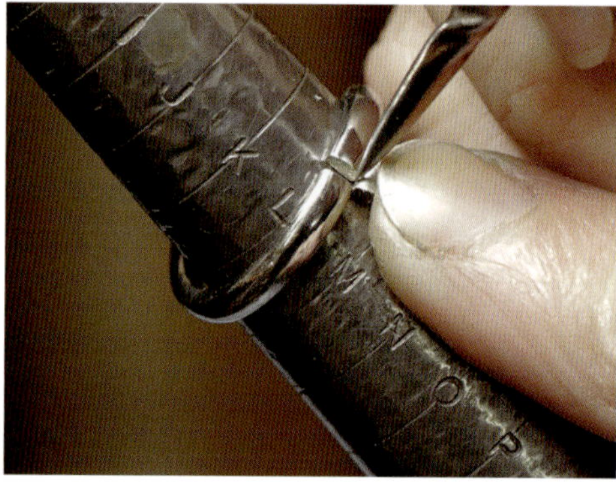

Measuring for the piece to be added to the ring.

Gently slide the ring off the mandrel, keeping the sizing stock in position. Make sure the joins are nice and flush. You will not be able to pass a saw blade through the joins just yet so make sure at least one of the joins is meeting lovely and flush.

Depending on how tight the tension is on the stock piece you may need to hold it in place using a pair of head and shank tweezers. If the ring contains any gemstones, then you will need to protect them with a good covering of a thermal paste barrier such as Cool Heat or Thermo-Gel. Cut a piece of 1,700-grade solder and have it ready to pick up.

Platinum does not need flux as it does not oxidise. Due to the high heat needed to melt the solder it is advisable to use an oxygen and propane torch or a water torch. Always use your platinum glasses to protect your eyes from the intense light caused by the heat of the torch.

Heat up the tweezers first, if you are using them, as they will act as a heat sink. Bring the flame towards your join. Do not use a solder pick as the point will contaminate the solder. Pick up the solder with a pair of fine-pointed tweezers and place on the solder join. You may need to hold it there whilst you heat it up in case the torch blows it off, as we do not have any flux to hold it in position.

Heat the join evenly until the solder flows. If both joins were perfectly flush then carry on and solder the other join. If this last join is not meeting square then allow it to cool and remove any thermal barrier paste. Pass a saw down through the join until the two ends come together perfectly.

Use the thermal barrier paste if needed and set up the ring in the head and shank tweezers again. We like to still use these on this join in case the previous solder join becomes molten. The tension of the ring shank will not force the piece out.

Cut a small pallion of 1700-grade platinum solder and heat the join. Solder in the same way as the first join. When cooled, remove the barrier paste, if used, and wash it off.

As with all platinum repairs, keep separate tools solely for platinum. Use your ring file that you keep just for platinum, to smooth down any excess on the inside of the ring. Do not file all the way down but stop just before you start to file the original ring. Swap over to a round buff stick or sanding drum to bring the stock piece you have added into alignment with the original ring metal. Put in onto your ring mandrel to check the size. If it is too big then start by cutting back through one of the joins and take as much metal out as needed and resolder. If the size is a little small then you can tap the stock metal you have added to make the ring the right size.

Once you have the ring the right size, start to file the outside of the ring shank so the new metal blends in with the original metal. Once this has been completed, start with a 600-grit emery paper sanding drum for the inside of the shank and a 600-grit emery buff stick for the outside. Work your way progressively through the grits, removing all the previous marks until you have reached at least 1,500 or 2,000-grit paper inside and outside the ring. If we do not carry out this step and stop on 600-grit, when we polish, the mops will drag out the solder in the join due to it being a little softer, as the solder is an alloy. This could cause slight grooves where the solder joins are.

When you have reached 1,500 or 2,000-grit emery paper, start to use a pre-polish on a polishing mop. Try to polish with the direction of the mop, perpendicular to the join so it is polishing across the join as opposed to polishing along it. This will help to stop the mop from dragging the solder out of the join. Once all the marks are off the metal, clean it in an ultrasonic. Use your final polish with soft cotton mops, inside and outside the ring shank. We should also be thinking of polishing the whole ring and not just the join, so emery and polish the whole shank.

Platinum is such a hard metal. The surface does not flow like gold and silver so when you polish, if there are any visible grit marks the polishing mops will not polish them out. The mops will polish the grit marks so the grooves will always be visible. That is why we need to go through all the grits of emery to leave a 'nearly' polished finish on the metal. Then when we come to use the polishing mops it will not take too long to produce that mirror shine.

Once you have used your final polish and put the piece through the ultrasonic, that is all that we need to do. Unlike white gold, platinum does not need rhodium plating. As the colour on the surface is the same colour all the way through the metal.

Using the head and shank tweezers to hold the piece in the shank whilst it is soldered.

REPAIRING RINGS WITH STONES

Removing Stones

There will come a time when you will have to remove gemstones from their settings and keep them in one piece. For example, you may need to re-tip or re-claw a setting that's holding a heat-sensitive stone.

Depending on how much wear the tips have, lifting them to remove the stone could well snap them off. This risk should have already been explained to the client at take-in and if they do indeed snap off, then a charge should be made to resolder them back into place. Alternatively, this scenario can be avoided by stating at the time of take in that if one or two claws need retipping, then it is advisable to have all the claws retipped at the same time so they are all of equal size.

You can buy claw lifting tools, which consist of slots in a rectangular piece of steel that can successfully lift claws without causing damage. This only works if the claws are not too worn, or flat to the stone.

A suitable size slot is selected for the claw. The sharp angled metal edge is placed at the join between the claw tip and the stone. The tool is levered back with pressure, keeping the sharp point in position. You do not necessarily have to pull the claw all the way back; this sometimes puts too much stress on the claw tip, causing it to fracture. Ease the claw up a little and repeat this on all the other claws. You may need to repeat this a few times, just enough to remove the gemstone.

Should the claw be worn down flat and you cannot get the claw lifter to stay in position, then you can try to slide a sharp scalpel blade between the tip and gemstone and ease the claw up. Always wear eye protection when carrying out this procedure in case the blade breaks. As this claw is very worn I expect we will be retipping, so it doesn't matter if it fractures. Care should be taken when using scalpel blades around gemstones, as scratching can easily occur.

If you have a pair of top cutters, you can use these in a similar way to the claw lifter. Rest one jaw just below the stone and the other at the junction between the tip and the stone. Pull back on the claw, levering against the lower jaw to lift the claw. Care has to be taken not to mark where this jaw is on the setting. Alternatively, an old pair of top cutters could be modified so the lower jaw has a rounded surface where the cutting edge was, to avoid marking the setting.

Claw lifting tool.

Using the claw lifting tool to raise a claw.

Easing a claw up using a scalpel blade.

Another way is to use a flat graver. The edge of this is always nice and sharp, and is ideal for lifting the claws. The angle of this cutting face is also ideal; it eases up the tip of the claw slowly, as the graver is pushed between the stone and the metal.

Tightening Claws

Over time, claws can become knocked from everyday wear and may lift slightly, leaving gemstones loose. If the claws are not tightened up then the tip of the claw may become caught, causing it to lift further, resulting in a lost stone, or even catching and ripping off the claw, losing the stone.

If the claw has sufficient thickness, then it should be able to be tightened against the stone successfully, however sometimes the claw has worn so thin that it offers no safety for the stone, in which case it would need to be built up.

We have two pieces of equipment for this, both inexpensive. A simple burnisher may be used to burnish and push the claw back onto the stone. Providing the tip of the burnisher is polished, then the surface of the tip will be burnished with a high polish too.

You can also use a beading tool to tighten the claw onto the stone. Select a beading tool with the cup the same size as the tip. With the ring in a ring clamp, gently put the beading tool onto the tip and gently push down with a twisting action. Be careful that the edge of the beading tool does not touch the stone, especially if the stone is a soft stone like opal, quartz, and the like. Rotate the tool and as the beading tool is polished, the tip of the claw will also be burnished by the rotating action of the beading tool.

A safety-edge file is a handy addition to your tool kit when working with claws. Let us show you how to make one. We are using a triangular file, but you can use a safety-back file as well. We do not want teeth on the edge of the file because when we come to clean up claws we want to run the edge of the file against the stone and if there are teeth on the edge, using the file could damage the stone and abrade the facets – even if the stone is a diamond.

Using a sharpening stone with a bit of oil, holding the tip and handle of your file, run the edge along the sharpening stone. You need to do this on all the edges to remove the teeth and make the edges smooth. If you have a fine sharpening stone, repeat this process to make these edges nice and smooth.

Lifting a claw with top cutters.

Lifting claw using a flat graver.

Tightening a claw using a burnisher.

Tightening claw using beading tool.

So now you are able to clean up the edges of claws using the teeth on the face of the file, but letting the edge (now without teeth) lightly run on the stone. There are still going to be limitations to this technique. If the stone is soft such as opal, turquoise or any stone less than 5 on the Mohs hardness table (*see* Appendix) then you may need to protect the stone with some tape, as the steel of the file may damage it. By angling the file, you should be able to round off the top of the claw ever so slightly. We are not looking to make the claw thinner but just tidy it up so that it is not sharp.

Another way to tighten claws onto a stone is to grind a thin groove down the inside of a pair of snipe-nose pliers.

Locate the claw that needs tightening up in the groove of one of the jaws, and clamp down with the other jaw under the setting, gently squeezing on the pliers.

Tightening claw using beading tool.

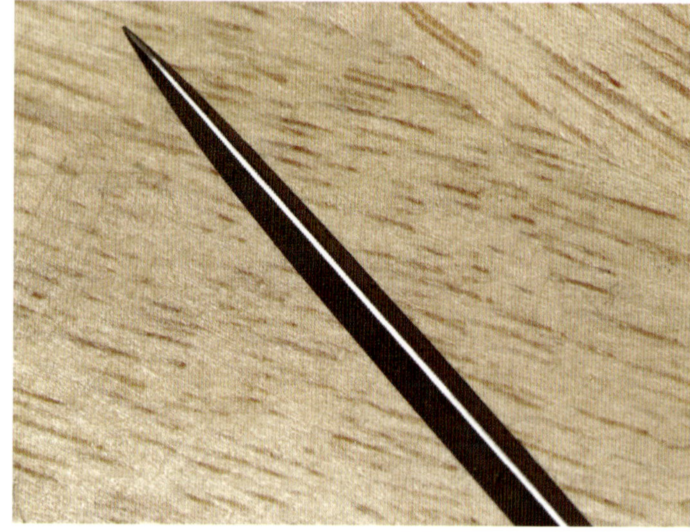
File showing the teeth on the edge.

Adding a little oil to a sharpening stone.

Rubbing the edge of the file on the sharpening stone to remove the teeth.

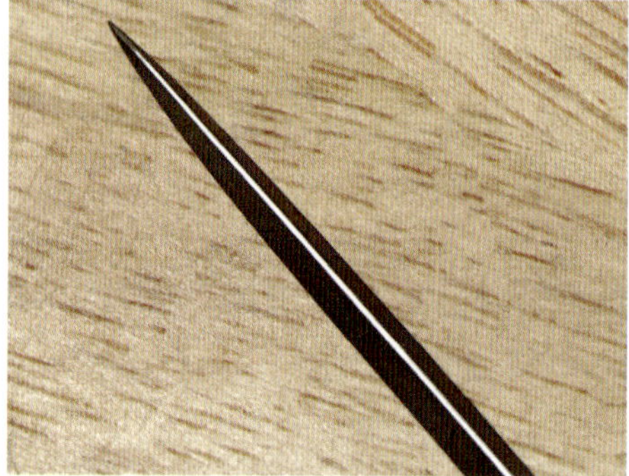
Safety-edge file with no teeth on the edge.

If the claws are all intact, are not worn and are all touching the stone, but the stone still turns in its seat, then you can tighten the claws using a pair of snipe-parallel pliers or snipe-nose pliers. Gently squeeze the two adjacent claws together slightly and then repeat on the opposite side. Then squeeze the claws back to their original position, but now tightened. By doing this you are easing the claws together so holding the stone tighter.

Retipping Claws

Some rings are worn every day, others only occasionally, but claws holding gemstones in place will always wear. The top of a ring comes into contact with things like door handles, cutlery, desks and clothing. This takes its toll on the tiny claws that may only be 1mm in size, or even less. As a result, claws are being constantly worn and over time they become very thin and flat, or they can catch on clothing, bend and get broken off. It is wise to educate the client to check on the condition of their ring at regular intervals. It is better to build up worn claws than to replace fractured ones, which could result in stone loss, which in turn causes distress and is a more costly repair for your client.

It is better to re-tip a claw than to replace it and there are a couple of ways we can approach this. We can re-tip when the top portion of the tip has worn flat or worn away, providing it has worn from the girdle of the stone and upwards. If the tip has worn flat and it is still covering the stone, we are able to rebuild the claw using solder matching the parent metal of the setting - this is often seen as a quick and cheap method as the solder is not as hard wearing as the actual metal. It is better to build up the claw using metal that matches the carat and colour of the setting.

Building up tips with solder

Sometimes this technique is frowned upon, but it's a great way to re-tip a claw, providing there is a bit of claw left over the stone. This technique can only be completed if the stone that's in need of re-tipping can withstand the heat of the torch – only diamonds and sapphires can be re-tipped this way. It is just too dangerous to do this with any other stone. It may be possible with rubies, but they are often treated to enhance the colour so this technique would ruin them. This is also unsuitable for any fracture-filled stones. If in doubt, take it out, particularly if it's a stone that you can't afford to replace.

Modified snipe-nose pliers with groove on inside.

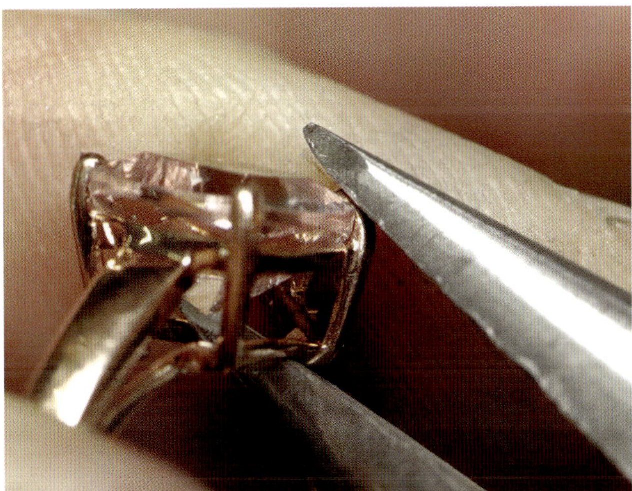

Using modified snipe-nose pliers to tighten claw.

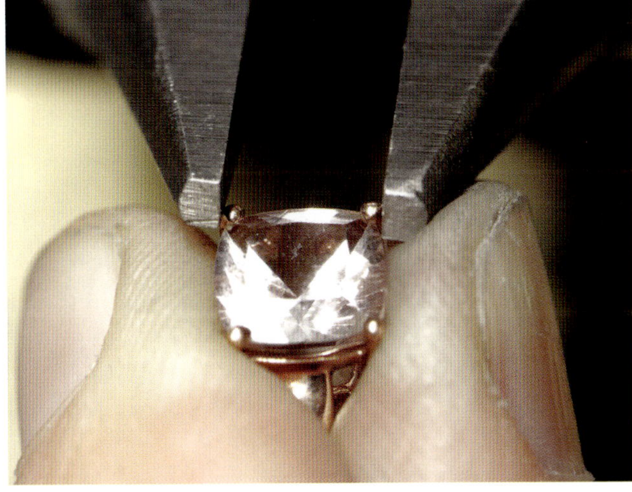

Easing claws together using snipe-parallel pliers.

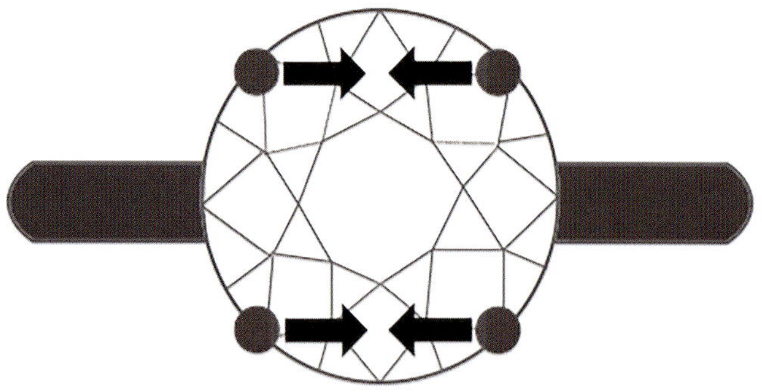 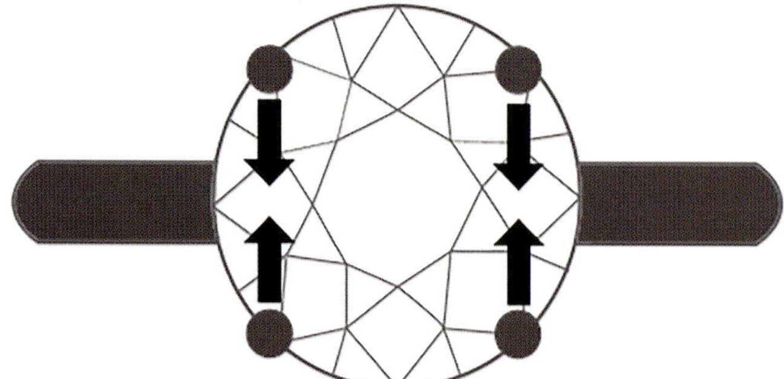

Direction of easing claws together to prevent stone turning.

Making sure the ring is absolutely clean before re-tipping.

The clean claw tip.

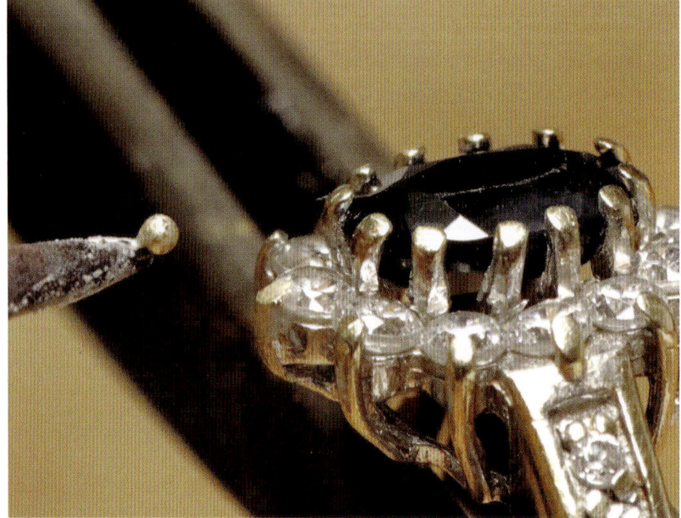

Adding a small ball of solder with the solder pick.

Melting the solder onto the claw tip.

The item that needs retipping must be absolutely clean. Make sure the item has been thoroughly cleaned, ensuring no dirt is trapped behind the stones, otherwise this will 'bake' onto the stones, and is very difficult to clean up afterwards.

Clean the tip of the claw by passing a file over the top of it. Try not to use emery paper as this is often made from carborundum, which will scratch the stones (except diamonds).

Using an easy solder of the same carat and colour of the tip you are building up, ball up a small pallion of solder on the end of your solder pick. We use easy solder as it melts at the lower temperature. If we tried to use medium or hard solder then we run the risk of other solder joins of the item coming apart.

The flame has to be small and not too hot. Direct the heat down on top of the worn tip, to melt the solder directly on top of it. If heat was directed lower down on the claw, then the solder will be inclined to follow the heat and run down the claw away from the tip.

Once the solder has flowed, remove the heat. This method needs minimal cleaning up if you have used the right amount of solder. A safety edge file can be used to blend the solder into the original claw. A rubber wheel, pumice wheel or bristle brush is then used to polish the claw and the areas between them.

Adding new metal to the tip

It is often advisable to remove the tip of the worn claw completely. This can be achieved by using a needle file to remove the tip down to the girdle of the stone.

Use some round wire, the same dimensions as the claws on the ring and of the same metal. File a flat on the end of this wire so it matches with the flat on the claw you have just filed.

Sweat-solder a tiny amount of easy solder onto the end of the wire.

With the ring held in a third hand, flux the filed claw and the soldered wire. Heat the ring up slowly bringing the flame towards the tip. Try to have a tiny flame here so we do not accidently heat up the other claws unnecessarily. Bring the wire into contact with the claw, direct the flame toward the claw but aim it slightly lower to heat up the basket as this will take longer to heat up than the wire. The solder will flow onto the claw from the wire.

The worn tip now built up.

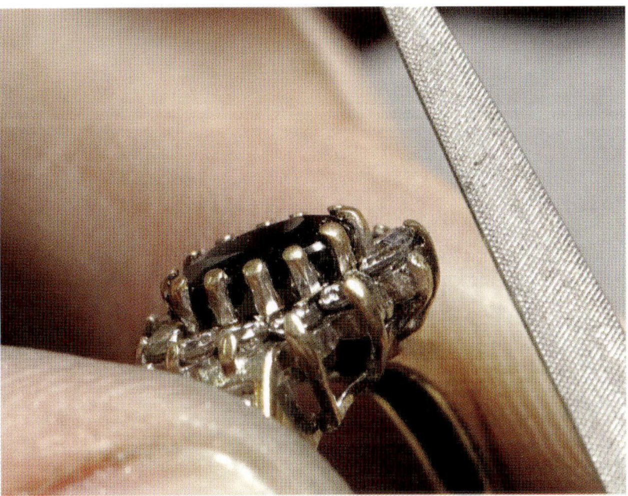

Filing the worn tip down.

Filing a flat on the new claw wire.

Sweat solder a small amount of solder on the end.

Aim the flame lower down to solder the wire onto the claw.

Snipping off the excess wire.

Wait for the ring to cool and cut off the excess wire.

Ease the new claw tip over onto the stone and file it into the same profile as the others using a safety edge file.

Using a rubber wheel, remove any file marks from the tip and blend it into the original claw.

You can use a beading tool of the correct size to push down the new claw tight onto the stone.

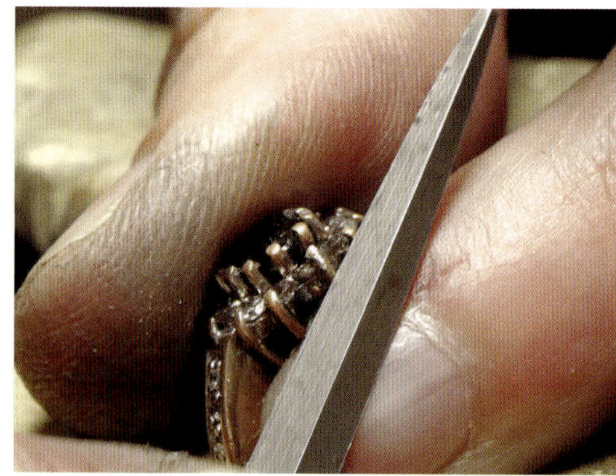
Filing the new claw to shape.

Cleaning up the new claw with a rubber wheel.

HANDLING HEAT-SENSITIVE STONES

If you are asked to re-tip claws that are holding heat-sensitive stones, it is wise to remove the stone and retip with the stone out of the setting. This can complicate the repair because the action of pulling the claws back to remove the stone could result in tips breaking off. This is a significant risk so it may be better to advise your client that all the tips would need to be replaced to be on the safe side. If the ring is old and has had considerable wear, the whole setting may be worn, so replacing the whole setting may be the best option from a cost perspective.

GENERAL RING REPAIRS

Soldering a Split Ring

There are several reasons why a ring shank may split or crack. We all know that metal such as silver and gold work-hardens: as the metal is moved then it gets harder and harder until it splits. This is also true of rings when worn. The back of the ring shank comes under constant pressure when worn and it is this minute moving of the metal that can cause the ring shank to split, especially if there is a solder join in that area. Solder is brittle compared with the parent metal and it is usually the first place to split. The shank can also split if the previous solder join was not prepared correctly. Perhaps the solder had not flowed all the way through the join or the item was quenched a little soon and caused the join to fracture. If the ring was originally cast, the casting may have been porous. Tiny air bubbles within the metal, when cast, make the metal weaker and the metal can simply crack when it is put under stress that's invisible to your client.

If you have such a repair, all the general soldering preparation needs to be carried out. It is not sufficient simply to add flux to the join and resolder. We need to pass a folded piece of emery paper through the split to ensure the join faces are clean of grease, dirt and oxides. If the split is open then a pillar needle file can be used and the join eased back together with a pair of half-round pliers until the join comes together perfectly parallel and level.

If the join has split and the ends of the join are slightly ragged, it is usually impossible to clean up the join faces with emery paper or a needle file, in which case a piercing saw can be passed through the join to remove any high spots and ensure a perfectly flat and parallel join. The ends will need to be adjusted and brought together tightly, even and level.

If there are gemstones or any other feature that would need protecting from the heat, place the ring upside down in some thermal barrier paste on a soldering block with the join uppermost. If the ring is plain, such as a wedding ring, it can simply be placed on a soldering block with the join facing away from you. Flux the join and cut a small pallion of solder to match the parent metal and colour.

Heat up both sides of the join to bring them to the same temperature at the same time. Add your solder to the join and continue to warm up the ring. If you see the solder move to one side, then direct the tip of the torch a little to the other side of the join. The solder will flow between the

Signet ring with fractured shank.

Using emery paper to clean and smooth the join.

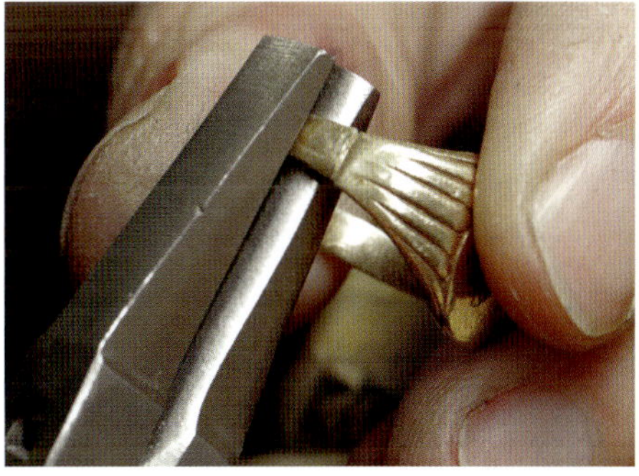

Bringing ends flush together.

Soldering the join.

Sanding and finishing.

Another issue identified to be rectified.

join. Turn the ring around and use the torch on the other side of the join and use the heat to 'pull' the solder all the way through to the other side of the join.

File and emery paper the join and polish in the usual way.

This particular ring has had a new shank put on it previously and upon further investigation we also noticed a slight split on the opposite side of the ring where the new shank was soldered on. In this scenario the best option would be to solder the original break, cut through the split on the opposite side, and resolder it.

Replacing Ring Shanks

Often when a ring comes in for repair, whether it is to have the ring shank soldered or resized, the actual metal is just too thin to make a satisfactory repair. It is in this instance that we need to think about a more serious repair. This type of repair is called a re-shank. This could be a quarter shank, where a small section is cut out and replaced, a half shank where half of the metal is removed and replaced or a full shank, removing the metal up to each shoulder or even removing the whole shank just leaving the original setting.

The idea here is to cut away the thin metal, removing as much as is needed to restore a nice width and thickness of metal. This may be cutting back to the original dimensions or just cutting back far enough to make a satisfactory repair. We are often asked to add thicker and wider metal than was originally present when it comes to a quarter or half shank. Whilst this is possible, personally I think it makes the ring look unsightly and really does not help to improve the strength of the ring, as although the piece of metal you solder into place is thick, you are still left with the thinner original metal that is weaker than the thick piece you have soldered into place.

So, the decision to replace a quarter, half or full shank may have already been decided for you. In which case, take a look at the ring and see if what is being requested is appropriate and will help improve the longevity of the ring. Will a quarter shank be suitable? Will the metal be thick and wide enough to make a successful repair and help improve the life of the ring? The same goes for a half and full shank.

Using a scribe or permanent pen, mark the area that you will be removing. Obviously, it is best not to remove the stamps on the inside of the shank so see if you can adjust the area to leave these intact. If you have to remove the markings, inform the client beforehand.

Before you start to remove the thin metal, try to measure the ring size. Hopefully this has been noted on the repair packet, or the size the ring has to be made to. If not, write down the ring size on the packet as determining the size of the ring once the shank has been cut off will not be very accurate.

Measure and record the ring size before starting work.

Now we have decided what we are going to remove, make sure that metal thickness is going to be the same at each point where we cut. Start to cut off the piece/pieces of ring shank and put them to one side. You may need to return them to the client.

With the pieces removed you can now measure the width and thickness of the piece of metal you need to put into the shank. Select a piece of stock metal that is a few tenths of a millimetre larger in each dimension. No point trying to solder on the exact size of metal as usually it needs to be filed into shape to blend in the join and this will make the metal thin again.

It is best to keep the metal stock a bit longer than is needed as it will be easier to bend the metal to the same curvature of the ring if we can hold onto it. Using either a pair of half-round pliers or a shank bender, ease the metal stock into a gentle curve to match the same curvature as the ring. This will make measuring the amount of metal we need easier. File the one end of the stock metal flat so it sits flush against one end of the metal left on the ring. Slide the ring onto your ring mandrel up to the correct size. Rest

Mark off the area you intend to replace.

Remove the old shank.

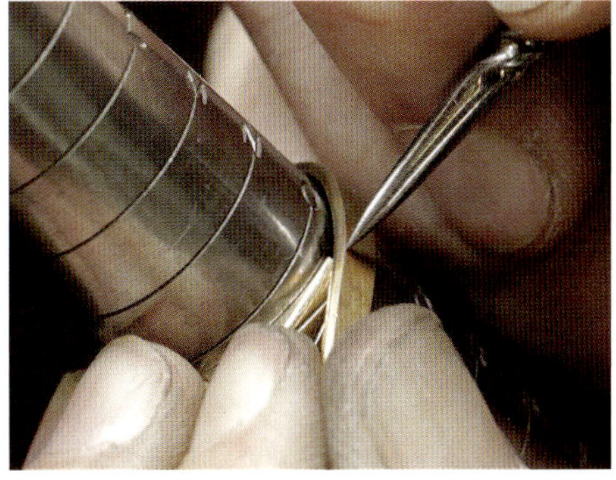

Mark off the correct length for the new piece.

Soldering the new shank in place.

Using head and shank tweezers to solder the new shank in place.

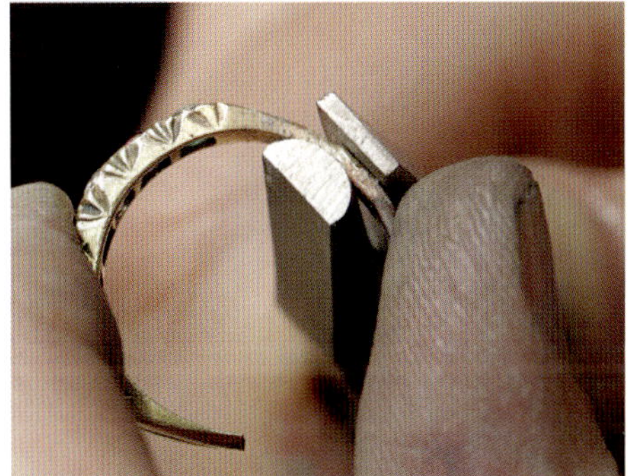

Shaping the new metal.

the filed end of your stock metal against one end and mark off where the opposite end of the cut ring shank is, making sure the stock metal is resting on the mandrel.

Cut on the waste side of this line. File it straight and offer up the new piece to the ring that is still on the mandrel. Does the piece fit into the gap? I would always make the new piece 0.25–0.5mm too small, knowing that we can gently tap the new piece a little to make it the correct size. If the piece is too big, then file one end back a little until the piece fits.

You can solder this new piece of ring shank into place in a couple of ways. One is to sweat-solder a piece of solder onto the end of the new piece of shank and holding it in your tweezers or third hand, bring it to the ring to be soldered.

Once this has been soldered into place you can adjust it so the other ends align perfectly and solder these together. If the first solder join was not perfect, you can cut through the solder join and resolder it accurately in place again.

The other method involves using a pair of head and shank tweezers and is great if you don't have a steady hand or want a bit more control. Place the ring into the head and shank tweezers with the head at the paddle end. Place the new piece of shank in position. Now you can align everything and the two pieces will be held in position by these tweezers. Flux the joins and solder them.

If there are heat-sensitive stones in the ring, protect these using a thermal barrier paste. This can be put all around the head of the ring and paddle end of the tweezers once the pieces have been assembled. If you have just soldered the one side, you can now remove the ring from the tweezers, align up the other side and carefully solder it. You should not need to put the ring back in the head and shank tweezers as the soldering on this other side should not cause the previous solder join to come undone.

Tidy up the inside of the ring with a ring file and size it on the mandrel. If the ring is a fraction too small, then tap the new piece of metal a little bit to bring the ring to the correct size. If it is too big, then a small piece will have to be cut out and that join resoldered.

Now you can file the new piece of metal to bring it into shape to match the rest of the ring shank. Emery and polish it to bring it back to showroom condition.

CHAPTER 5

ATTACHING AND REPAIRING CLASPS

REPLACING BOLT RINGS

It is always a good idea to stock a few different sizes of bolt rings: 5mm, 6mm and 7mm. Anything larger than this can be bought in as and when needed. They are often available in standard and heavy weight. I usually stick with the standard weight and I always buy closed-ring bolt rings. This refers to the joining ring on the clasp. You can buy open ring clasps but I find that when you need to solder that ring closed, you often damage the spring in the clasp which makes it unusable. Buy closed and if you need it open then you can simply use your piercing saw. If closed, you can easily attach it to the chain with another small jump ring and be able to solder that jump ring closed, as it's further away from the clasp and it can be soldered without damaging the spring.

Remove the old clasp if it is still present and choose a similar sized clasp if a specific size has not been requested.

Some jewellers always solder on the bolt rings, others simply twist them closed. There is no wrong or right way although for safety and security I would always solder the bolt ring on.

If you are very good at soldering you may be tempted to solder an open-ring bolt ring once it has been attached to the chain, but the problem is that the heat generated by the torch could take the temper from the spring and make it useless.

I prefer to take a bolt ring with a closed jump ring and attach it to the chain with a small 2mm or 3mm jump ring. This way the bolt ring can be positioned out of the way to avoid it being heated up. Thermal protective paste can also be placed around the bolt ring to avoid too much heat getting conducted to the spring.

If you have access to a pulse welder or laser welder then you will be able to join up the open jump ring attached to the bolt ring. Using this equipment will not damage the spring in the bolt ring as no general heat is passed through to it.

Broken bolt ring.

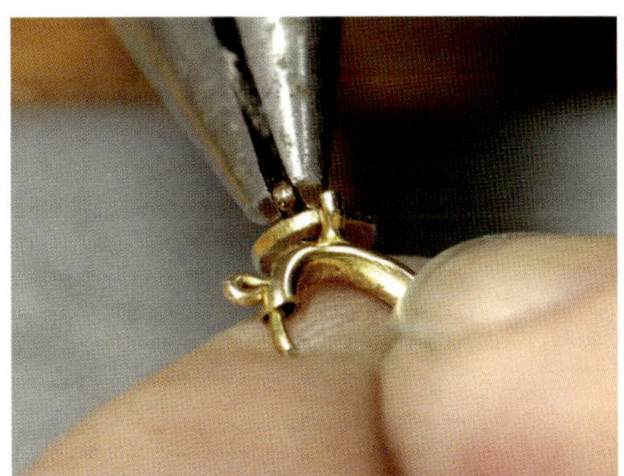

Removing the old bolt ring.

Soldering the bolt ring.

OPPOSITE: Soldering on a new clasp.

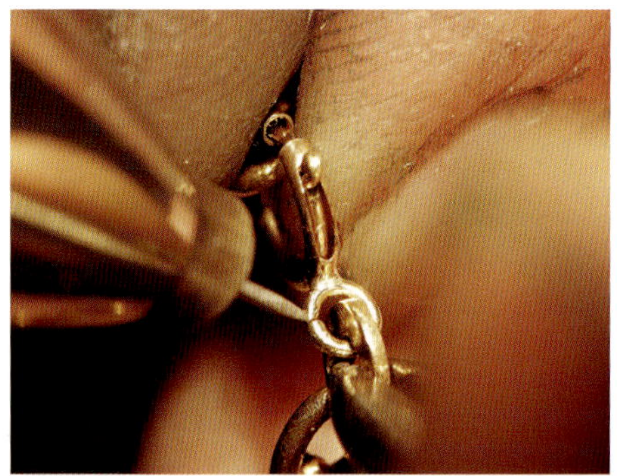

A pulse welder will not heat-damage the spring.

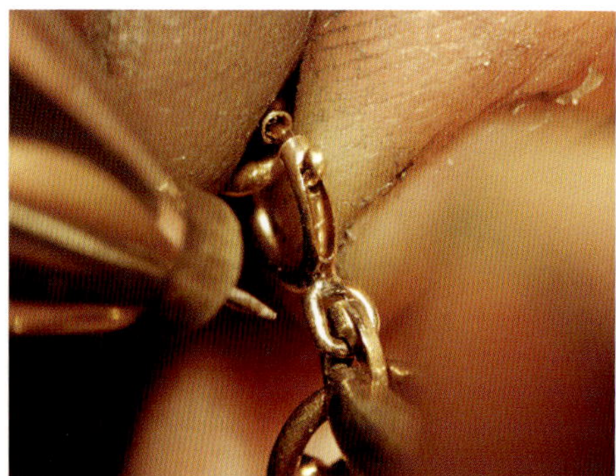

Using a pulse welder to secure the bolt.

Lobster clasp in 3rd hand, positioned away from solder area.

REPLACING TRIGGER CLASPS

Trigger, lobster and parrot clasps may all look slightly different but they all play the same part. These clasps are thicker and heavier than bolt rings so they are usually used on heavier or higher-carat chains. Due to their manufacture, they are solid as opposed to hollow (like bolt rings) so they wear better and last longer. The only downside is that they are more costly, but their longevity and durability outweigh the cost.

ALWAYS USE A ROUND JUMP RING

When attaching clasps to chains, always use a round jump ring instead of an oval one. If a round jump ring is used and allowed to turn freely, it will rotate, allowing even wear around the ring and it will last longer.

Oval jump ring adjacent to lobster clasp.

When you purchase these clasps, they do not usually have the attaching jump ring to attach to the chain, so you would also need to provide one of these. Something to consider with your pricing. It is wise to replace this jump ring as it is often worn, but if it's in good condition then by all means, reuse it.

The attaching jump ring is often soldered so care must be taken to avoid getting the lobster clasp hot from the flame, or you will end up ruining the spring in the clasp. Either protect the clasp with a thermal paste barrier or arrange the chain on your soldering block or in a third hand with the clasp out of the flame's path, so you can safely solder the jump ring.

REPLACING PEARL AND BEAD CLASPS

When a broken bead or pearl clasp arrives at your bench there are a few details we have to look out for. Why has the clasp broken? Is it because the strand has been pulled? If that is the case, is the integrity of the thread still intact? Has the thread broken at the end where the clasp is fastened? Has the clasp simply worn out? This could be due to wear and tear. Look at the rest of the strand, has the thread stretched, causing gaps between the beads?

If you are in any doubt as to the condition and integrity of the thread, then suggest the necklace be rethreaded and at the same time a new clasp can be fitted.

If the thread looks in good condition, inspect the end where the clasp attaches. If they are heavy beads or pearls, then there should be a small spiral of metal around the thread forming the loop where the clasp attaches. This spiral of wire is called 'French wire' and its job is to protect the thread from wearing away. This French wire is added to the thread when the pearls have been strung so if it is missing or worn through, then the necklace will have to be rethreaded and a new clasp added at the same time.

A typical pearl clasp comprises two pieces. A decorative body and the other piece is folded over a long U-shape. This is the part that often breaks, as the action of it going into the decorative body half and squeezed to remove it leads to this breaking, usually from work-hardening of the metal.

So, assuming the clasp has broken, which is usually the case, we should be able to remove it, either by using top or side cutters. If both pieces of the clasp need replacing, then we can remove the two sides, otherwise we can simply remove the broken half. If it is the U-shaped piece, this can be replaced if you are able to get one to match.

New clasps can be added easily by removing the old clasp and using small jump rings to reattach the new parts. You will have to make sure the French wire, if there is any, is intact. If there is no French wire to protect the thread, then it is wise to consider rethreading the necklace and adding new French wire at the same time.

REPAIRING THE TONGUE OF A CLASP

If the U-shaped part of the clasp is made from silver or gold, and if you have both parts, you could solder it back. Otherwise, you can always solder on a piece that matches the part that has broken off. Remember to work harden the U-shape end to ensure the clasp will repeatedly work.

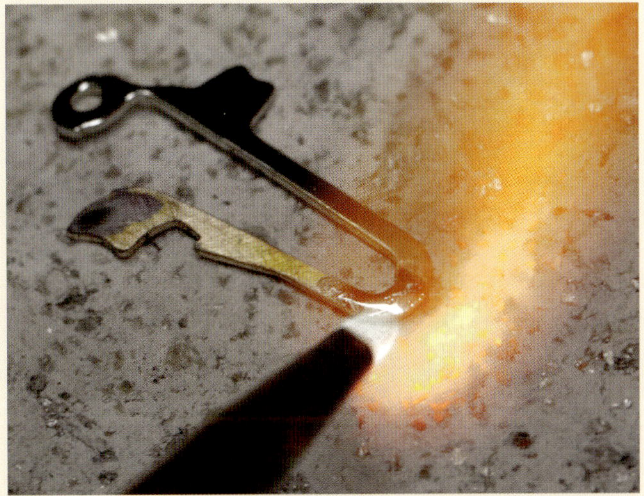

Soldering a clasp.

Pearl necklace with broken thread.

A typical pearl clasp.

A pearl clasp attached with jump rings.

CHAPTER 6

REPAIRING EARRINGS

REPLACING RIVETS

We do not often see rivets in jewellery as most of the joins are soldered, but the one place we see rivets is on earrings fittings.

Creoles are a popular style of earring and one that indeed has a rivet which acts as a hinge between the body of the earrings and the ear wire to enable the earrings to be hung from the ear.

Sometimes the rivet comes out or breaks, so being able to make this repair is beneficial to make the earrings wearable again.

If the rivet is still in place and has worn, then a fine pair of tweezers or snipe-nose pliers can be used to ease the old rivet out, taking care not to bend the thin end of the ear wire. Choose a piece of wire the same metal as the earring that just fits into the hole of the hinge.

File a flat on the end of the wire and then use a small ball pein or cross pein hammer to 'mushroom' over the one end of the wire. This can be achieved by fastening the wire in a small vice leaving approximately 1mm above the jaws of the vice. Any higher and the wire will bend when it is hit with the hammer. Lightly tap the end of the wire straight on to form a rivet head. This has to be wider that the wire to prevent the rivet sliding out.

Once that has been done, place the ear wire in the join on the earrings and pass the wire through, making sure the rivet head is tight against the outside of the join. Using a pair of flush cutters, snip the wire close to the join leaving approximately 0.5–0.75mm.

Creole earring with missing rivet.

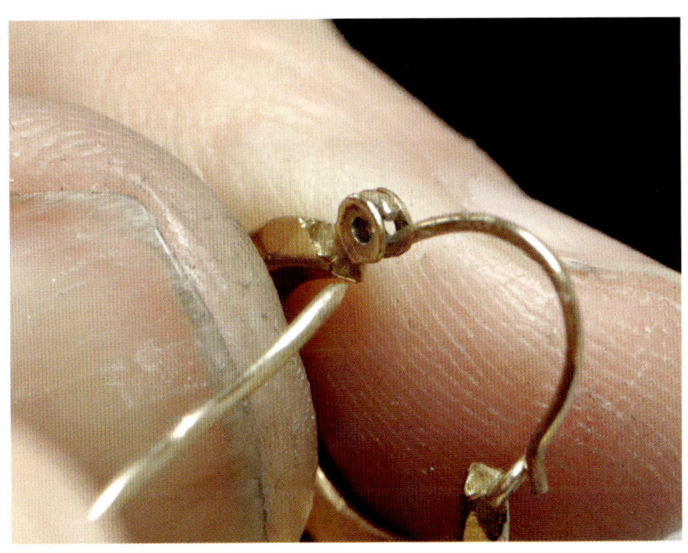

Choosing suitable wire for the replacement rivet.

OPPOSITE: Soldering an ear post on.

Forming the rivet head.

Adding new rivet to earring.

Riveting the opposing side.

Place the riveted side of the wire on a steel block and using the same technique you just used, hammer the end of this piece of wire. The steel block will stop the wire from moving and you should be able to 'mushroom' over the other end of the wire. You still want to be able to move the ear wire when you have finished riveting so do not hammer the rivet down hard.

Gently clean each head of the rivet with a piece of emery paper and polish both earrings to bring them up to an 'as new' finish.

SOLDERING EARRING POSTS

Often an earring post happens to snap off. This usually happens because the point of contact between the end of the post is far too small to make a sufficient solder join. Earrings posts are often 0.8mm round wire and with all the pushing, pulling and stress that these posts take either the posts snap, or the solder joins become brittle and they snap.

When you are confronted with this repair, you need to ascertain if the earrings are of a metal that can be soldered, for example, silver or gold. Secondly you have to see what the earring is. Does it have any stones set in it? How are they set? What stones are they? Can they take the heat? Is there any enamel or resin decoration on the earring? All of these questions will ultimately determine if the earring can be repaired by soldering on a new earring post.

Often these earrings contain heat-sensitive stones, and they cannot be removed to enable the post to be soldered on. Even using a thermal barrier paste, it's still not possible to solder the post on if the stones are too close to the area being soldered.

So, assuming that all is good and we are able to solder the post on, we need to remove the old post if there is a piece still attached. This can be done with a ball burr. This burr is more favourable than a file as there is less likelihood of marking the rest of the back of the earring.

Once this has been removed, we need to think about making the solder join a stronger one. There are a couple of ways to do this. Get yourself a 1.5mm ball burr and use it to make a divot at the point you wish to solder the

Stud earring with fractured post.

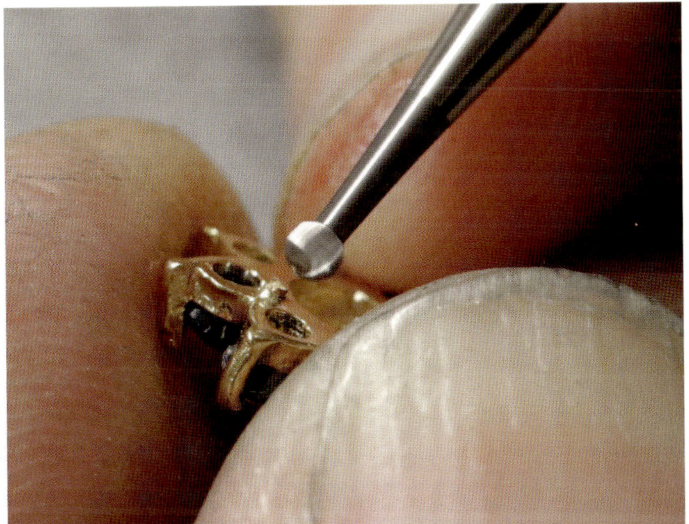

Removing residual post from earring.

Increasing the surface area to be soldered using ball burr.

Sweating solder onto post end.

Post in situ and soldering.

Balling up the post end to increase its surface area.

post. Go down to half the depth of the burr, for example, approximately 0.75mm.

Then place a tiny pallion of solder on your soldering block and sweat-solder it onto the end of an earring post.

Using your tweezers, take your new earring post with some flux on the end (making sure you know which way around these posts go) and as you heat up the earring to the point where the solder melts, bring the post into place and keep the flame off the post or it will melt. As soon as the solder melts bring the end into the divot. Remove the flame and hold the post still until the solder solidifies. If you move the post too soon you may get a fracture at the join that will separate later on. By using this technique, you have increased the surface area of the post that is in contact with the earring.

The other way to increase the area of the portion of the post in contact is to obtain a slightly longer post than is needed or indeed make one yourself of the correct diameter wire. Using a small hot flame, melt a small ball from the end of the post and then file half of the ball off. This gives the post a larger base on which to solder.

Flux and melt a small amount of solder onto the flat area that you have just filed. Clean the area on the earring that you are going to solder. Clean the post and add some flux. Heat up the earring and as the metal increases in heat, bring the post down to where it needs to be soldered. Again, keep the flame off the post and as the post comes into contact with the earring, the heat from the earring transfers to the post bringing the post up to the temperature of the earring. As they both achieve the correct temperature for the solder to flow, the post will be soldered securely to the earring.

Putting a flame on an enclosed hollow item such as a ball earring is very dangerous. If the hollow item is heated up the air inside expands quickly. If it has no way to escape then the hollow item will explode. To avoid this happening, it is advisable to use a tiny drill (approximately 0.5mm diameter) to open a hole that will not be noticeable from the front of the earring. This will allow the air to escape when the post is soldered on.

Drilling a discrete hole to allow escape of air during soldering.

Soldering post onto hollow earring with air release hole drilled.

CHAPTER 7

REPAIRING BRACELETS

ADDING SAFETY CHAINS

Safety chains are added as a security measure on bracelets and bangles, just in case the clasp breaks or comes undone. Should that happen the safety chain stops the bracelet or bangle from falling off the wrist.

The length of standard safety chains is 65–75mm, but you are able to make the chains at whatever length you need.

Safety chain repairs can include the following:

1. The most obvious is that the safety chain needs to be repaired just like any other simple chain. This is a straightforward chain repair, which we have covered in the chain repair section.
2. One of the adjoining jump rings that fasten the chain to the bracelet may need soldering or replacing – this should be a straightforward repair. Often these jump rings are not soldered, so it is best to solder them.
3. The other type of repair is where there is a small jump ring soldered onto the bracelet and the safety chain fastens onto this. As these jump rings are soldered, they often snap off or become worn, so it is wise to replace them. Let us see how that is carried out.

Firstly, we need to take off the old jump ring. Lay the bracelet out on your soldering block and add a little flux to the solder join. This facilitates the solder flow and leaves the area where we remove the jump ring from nice and smooth. Warm up the link or the area that this jump ring is soldered to, and try not to direct the heat onto the jump ring as it will usually melt due to its size. Take hold of your tweezers and just as the solder holding the jump ring on starts to melt take hold of the jump ring and remove it. Let the bracelet cool and pickle just the end link you have heated up.

Sweat-solder a small amount of solder where the old jump ring was. This makes it easier when soldering it onto the bracelet as you will not have to try to juggle a pallion of solder while holding the tweezers and also holding the torch.

Using a jump ring of the same metal and size, add a little flux to the area you've sweat-soldered, and onto the jump ring. Hold the jump ring in tweezers with the join facing towards the bracelet, warm up the bracelet link and then just before the old remains of solder start to melt bring the new jump ring into place. Do not direct the torch onto this jump ring as it will melt. Let the jump ring touch the bracelet link and let it heat up. When the solder on the bracelet link flows, the jump ring should be the same temperature and so the solder joins the two. Remove the torch and allow to cool. Place in the pickle to clean.

I would clean up the bracelet now before adding the safety chain as chains can get caught in the polishing mops. Polish and ultrasonic the bracelet and dry. Now add a small jump ring to attach the safety chain to the link we just soldered to the bracelet. Hold this jump ring in a third hand and flux the join. Cut a small pallion of appropriate solder. Heat up the jump ring and solder it closed keeping the safety chain out of the way to avoid it being soldered to the jump ring.

OPPOSITE: Charm bracelet.

Removing the old jump ring.

Sweat solder onto the link.

Solder the new jump ring to the pre soldered link.

Attaching and soldering the safety chain.

Cleaning up with a small scratch brush.

Attaching a safety chain to the bracelet link.

Soldering closed.

Clean using a scratch brush.

Allow to cool and clean up the jump ring using a brass scratch brush to avoid the chain tangling in the polishing motor.

If there are no fixed jump rings to solder a safety chain onto then one can easily be added to a bracelet. Using the jump rings that usually come fitted with the safety chains, loop these around any open links near to the clasp.

Due to the size of this jump ring, we are using paste solder but equally, pallion solder and flux can be used. Use a third hand to hold the link clear above the rest of the bracelet. Heat up this jump ring gently, bringing the flame down from the top to avoid putting any direct flame on the bracelet itself.

The safety chain is quite fine, so we opt for a brass scratch brush and warm soapy water to clean the job. This is a great way to clean silver charm bracelets too.

REPAIRING A PADLOCK HASP

A padlock is an old-fashioned type of clasp often used to secure charm bracelets. There are not many parts of a padlock to go wrong and often the hasp, the top piece that moves, is the part that breaks. It can either wear out on either side of the hasp due to the constant wear of the adjoining large jump rings, (often seen on Victorian or Edwardian items), or the thumbpiece breaks off.

If the thumbpiece has broken off, it can be replaced rather than replacing the whole hasp, providing the rest of the hasp is not too worn.

Start off by selecting a section of metal, usually round wire, to match the existing hasp. Clean the area to be soldered on the original hasp.

You may need to file the end of the new thumbpiece to match the shape of the broken one so we will be able to make a seamless appearance once the hasp has been polished.

Flux the area and solder the ends together, being careful to align the ends precisely.

Bend the thumbpiece into alignment so it is close fitting to the original hasp and cut it level with the top of the loop of the hasp. Smooth off this cut end.

Holding the hasp in a pair of parallel pliers, make a wide cut a few millimetres up from the soldered end of the hasp to catch into the body of the padlock and then also make three more cuts with your piercing saw about 1/4 of the way through the wire, so your finger can grip the end to open the clasp.

Adjust the shape of the hasp so it catches into the padlock body. Clean and polish the hasp and the rest of the padlock to finish.

Silver padlock with fractured thumbpiece.

Selecting appropriate wire for the repair.

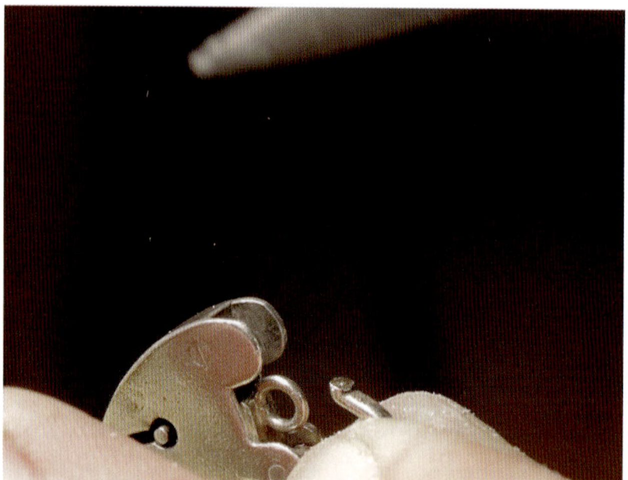

Filing a new piece to match up the shape.

Soldering together.

Bending thumbpiece into alignment.

Adding grooves.

Replacing a Worn Padlock Hasp

If the hasp has worn, it's best to replace it with a new one. You may be able to build up the worn areas with solder, but that's not the best type of repair, and it is often false economy to carry out the repair in this way. The solder is less hard-wearing than the original metal and will wear through at a quicker rate. Replacing it is straightforward, as you are able to buy a variety of different-sized hasps from suppliers.

The hasps are simply riveted into place so to remove the old one, start by filing off the rivet head at the back of the padlock. We choose to do this on the back as we might mark the front of the padlock, and this padlock that we're working on has fine engraving on the front.

Tap out the old rivet using a flat-headed punch, or you can use an old burr with the cutting head snapped off and filed flat with a diamond wheel. Support the padlock whilst doing this.

Grab the head of the rivet with a pair of flat-nose tweezers. Twist it and pull it out.

Measure the diameter of the old rivet and select a new piece of wire of the same diameter. With approximately 1mm of the new wire above the jaws of a vice, use a ball pein hammer to mushroom over the end of the wire.

This rivet head will be at the front of the padlock so the head needs to be nice and round. Use a needle file to shape the rivet head.

File a slight taper on the opposite end of the wire and put the hasp into place. Gently tap the new wire from the front of the padlock.

Tap the wire into position using a large beading tool. This will help to round off the front of the rivet.

Leaving approximately 1mm of rivet protruding out of the back of the padlock, use a ball pein hammer to mushroom over the wire. Support the padlock whilst doing this. If you do this on a metal block, you may need to reshape the front rivet head with the beading tool again.

Check the hasp can move. It needs to be opened so make sure you have not riveted it too tightly. Clean and polish the whole padlock to bring it back as new.

Punching out the old rivet.

Filing off the old rivet head.

Pulling out the old rivet.

Put the new rivet in a vice to start mushrooming over the end.

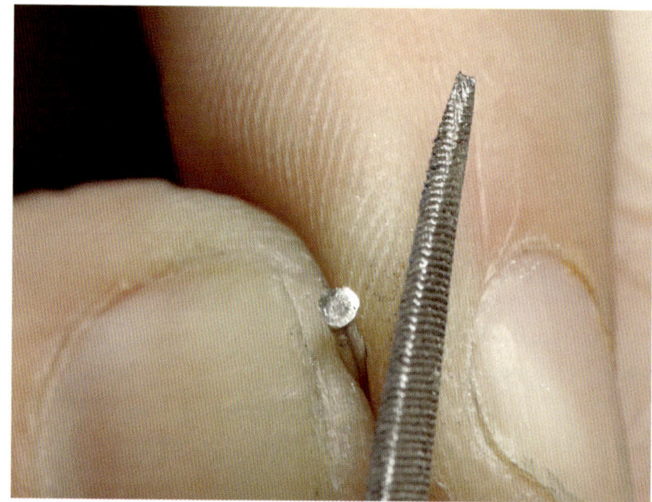

Tidying up the mushroomed end to make it round.

Tapping the new rivet into the padlock.

Rounding off the head of the new rivet.

Riveting over the end of the wire.

Cleaning the rivet heads and padlock.

REPAIRING A TONGUE CLASP

Box clasps are often used in larger and more expensive bracelets, bangles and chains as a means of fastening. A tongue is attached onto one end of the chain and on the other end is a box that the tongue goes into. This tongue is made from a folded piece of metal, usually white gold if the item is gold, with a small thumbpiece soldered onto it. Due to the action of the tongue going into the box and becoming compressed, the folded over edge becomes work hardened over time and eventually it can crack or split and fall off. So, we need to solder this back into place.

We have to lift up the opposite end of the tongue to avoid it becoming soldered flat and closed, this would make the clasp useless. Clean the area of both parts of the tongue to be soldered.

Using a piece of steel or titanium (these metals will not be affected by the silver or gold solder), lift the one edge and have the split ends in contact with each other. Flux this area.

Either hold the end of the thumbpiece in your third hand or lay it on your soldering block. Bring your torch flame along with a piece of easy solder to match the metal of the clasp you're working on.

Fractured box clasp.

Cleaning both parts with emery.

Lift one edge and have the split ends in contact with each other.

Thumbpiece in third hand.

Concentrating heat on lower (largest) part first.

Encourage solder to flow across the join.

Tapping the soldered tongue on a steel block.

Try not to concentrate the flame on the small part of the tongue you are soldering back on. As this is smaller than the rest of the end of the clasp, it is likely to melt. Concentrate your flame onto the lower part to heat this up first.

As the top piece of the clasp you are soldering on is in contact with the rest of the tongue, it will heat up to the required temperature. The solder is brought into position on the join, and just as the temperature is right, the solder will flow along the join. Move the torch along the join to encourage the solder to flow along to the other end.

The tension will have been taken out of the tongue due to the heat from soldering, so we need to introduce a bit of work hardness in the tongue to make it springy. Put the end of the tongue on a steel block and using a flat faced hammer, tap the join a few times. This will introduce a bit of tension in the metal. Open up the tongue clasp a little to see if it has some tension – it should be springy. Try it into the box side of the clasp and adjust the tongue accordingly. Finish off the join with emery paper and polish it up.

REPLACING A FIGURE OF 8 CLASP

Along with box clasps you will sometimes find what is called a 'figure of 8' clasp on one or both sides of the clasp. These are there to add extra security to the box clasp should the clasp thumbpiece be accidentally pressed and the clasp comes undone, or the tongue wears loose and flattened, thus rendering the clasp ineffective.

It is called a 'figure of 8' clasp because the small wire that acts as the catch is similar in shape to a number 8. The components are a small tube with thin wire through it and a small ball that this wire in the shape of a figure of 8 catches onto.

Sometimes the tube wears away due to constant use over time, which ultimately wears away the figure of 8 wire too, so these two parts would need to be replaced. The old tube would need to be removed with a file, or by unsoldering it, and the new tube soldered into place – making sure when the clasp is done up the wire fits tightly over the end ball of the catch.

Bangle with missing 'figure of 8' clasp.

Applying rouge to act as a solder inhibitor.

Rouge

We use some rouge powder mixed with a drop of water and a little bit of soap to break down the surface tension of the water. This is applied with a fine paint brush.

Correction Fluid

Not used as often these days but try to use the water-soluble mixture as the spirit base in some brands is dangerous when heated and inhaled. Simply paint it on the areas you do not want the solder to flow.

Graphite

A soft leaded pencil is ideal as this can be simply drawn onto the chosen area to stop the flow.

Yellow Ochre Paint

Some of this paint when mixed with a drop of water can be painted onto the protected areas to halt the flow of solder.

All of these methods of stopping the solder from flowing can be washed off in water or the pickle.

Inserting the wire through the tube.

Care must also be taken to avoid the solder flowing into the tube and onto the thin wire when the tube is soldered onto the bracelet. This can be avoided by using powdered rouge mixed with a drop of water, applied to the area where you do not want the solder to flow.

To fit a new wire, we simply remove the old one if it is still in place and select a piece of wire of the same metal as the previous wire – approximately 35–40mm in length. The wire is usually 0.8mm diameter.

The wire is passed through the tube half-way. It is then folded over, so the two ends come together evenly and overlap slightly.

This wire is then brought up to the ball on the other end of the bracelet, bangle or necklace and adjusted so it just passes over it with no resistance.

The crossed end of the wire is hung over the side of a soldering block and fluxed. A hot flame is directed towards the ends of the wire and feathered on and off. The idea is to melt these ends of the wire together.

Once melted, quench in the pickle and tidy up the balled end with a file and buff stick. Put the clasp together and fold the wire over the end ball. Using a pair of round-nose pliers on either side of the wire, gently squeeze the wire into a loose figure of 8 shape. This will close the wire around the end ball slightly.

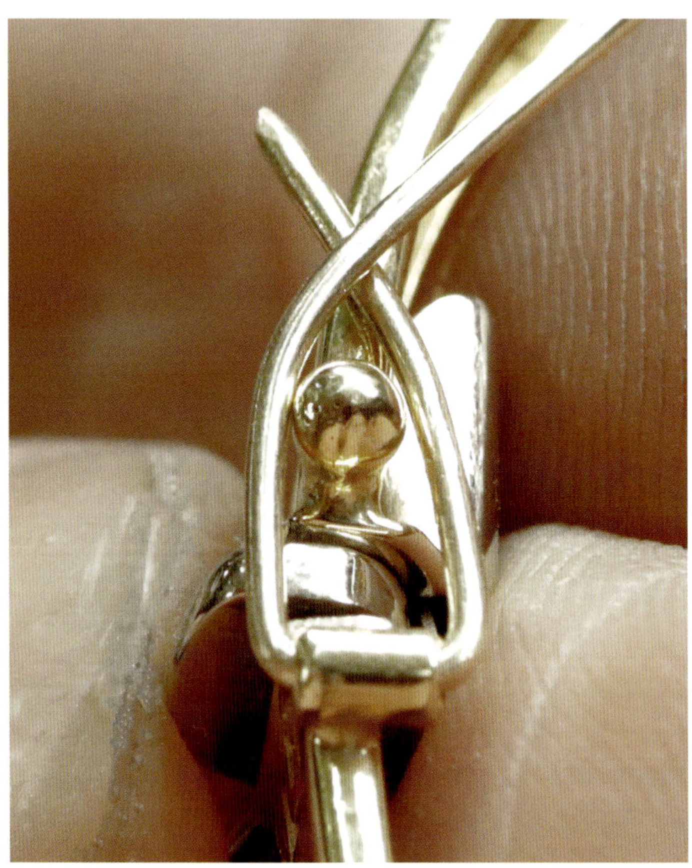

Bending the wire into a U-shape.

Unclip the clasp and lift up the melted ball end slightly so a fingernail can be located behind it to help release it. Finish up the clasp with a pre-polish and then a final polish.

Easing it around the ball catch.

Melting the ends of the wire together.

Easing the wire into shape.

Polishing with a bristle brush.

CHAPTER 8

MISCELLANEOUS REPAIRS

SOLDERING A JUMP RING

This is one of the most basic techniques that everyone needs to master. It is used in so many ways from repairing chains, soldering on safety chains, catches and adding charms to bracelets.

In this job, we are soldering on a charm to a gold charm bracelet.

Choose a jump ring of a similar size to the others on the bracelet and open it up. Put the charm onto it and thread it onto the bracelet. It is important to note that the charms must be placed along the bracelet evenly where possible and also the right way around as nearly all charms have a front and back. This has to correspond with any other charms already soldered onto the bracelet.

You can lay the jump ring on your soldering block or hold it in your third hand. I like to use a third hand as the heat that will be conducted through the link will stop at the tweezers, whereas if it was on a soldering block, the heat could travel through to the bracelet and cause it to discolour. Use some solder paste, which is great for small jump rings like this or a small pallion of solder and flux.

The jump ring shouldn't need much cleaning up. You can do this using a small mop in your flex shaft or micromotor. A quick dip in the ultrasonic is all that is needed.

Charm bracelet with charm to be soldered on.

OPPOSITE: Soldering on a pearl post.

Choosing a suitable jump ring.

Soldering the jump ring with bracelet in a third hand.

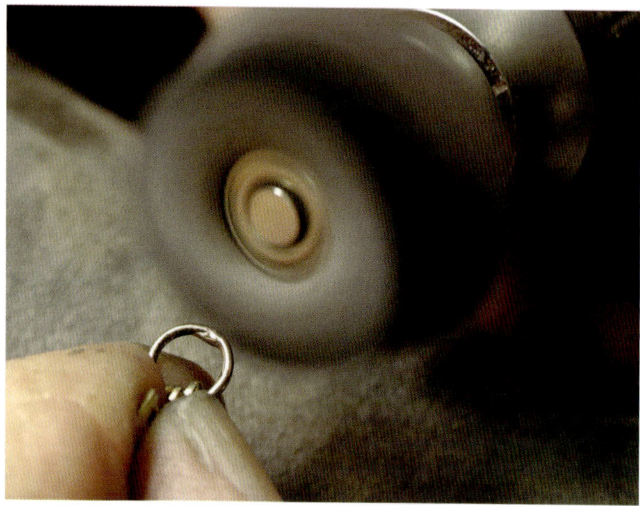
Cleaning up the jump ring with a mop.

SHORTENING A CHAIN

When a client buys a chain, it often comes in set sizes but if the client needs it slightly smaller to fit then we are able to remove links to make the fit better. This is often carried out on bracelets because if the bracelet is too big, it is likely to slip over the wrist and become lost.

Start by measuring the wrist and working out how many links need to be removed to make it the correct size. Cut through one of the original joins on the first and last link of the section that needs to be removed.

Twist the links apart, remove the unwanted section and reassemble the chain.

Making sure the join is tight, flux the area and solder using an easy solder and quench in safety pickle to remove the oxides.

If the links are able to be held and you are careful, use a flex shaft on a slow speed to clean up the soldered link.

Depending on the size of chain, a quick going over with a brass brush may be all that the chain needs to clean it. A polish on a mop may be required if the link is larger, taking all the precautions previous discussed into consideration.

Cutting through original join.

Twist apart, shorten and reassemble.

Flux, solder and pickle.

Cleaning up the soldered link.

Cleaning the chain with a brass brush.

CEMENTING PEARLS AND BEADS

There is often only one way to fasten a pearl or bead. Usually, the pearl or bead is half-drilled, meaning that there is a small hole typically 0.8mm–1mm in diameter on one side. The pearl or bead is then attached to the item on a short peg, held into place with pearl cement. The peg is often serrated or twisted to provide a key for the adhesive.

Take a quick look over the rest of the item. See if any other part of it needs repair. If it is a brooch, check the workings of the pin, hinge and clasp. If it is a pendant then look at the bail to see if there is any wear that could benefit from being built up before we reattach the pearl. Also take a moment to polish the item too, as it will be easier to do now, without the pearl in place.

If an item comes in for repair with the pearl or bead missing, look to see why it has come off. Has the peg snapped off from the item? Or has the pearl simply come unstuck? The cement may have dried up, and the peg is still fastened to the item.

If the pearl has simply come unstuck, all you need to do is to remove any residual cement from the peg with a knife, or needle file if it is stubborn. Make sure the peg has some roughness about it, again use the needle file to create a few grooves if it's quite smooth. Then we need to remove any old cement from inside the hole. Put a drill of a similar size to the hole into a pin vice and twist it as you insert it into the hole. By doing so, the drill will pull out any remaining cement within the hole.

Next, check that the pearl fits onto the peg and goes all the way down. If not, drill the hole a little more and check again. Once you are happy with the fit, apply some pearl cement into the hole or on the peg and carefully slide the pearl onto the peg, being careful to avoid any excess cement going onto the pearl. A little piece of tissue paper is great to gently wipe away any excess as you ease the pearl down onto the peg. Leave the item in an upright position for a few hours for the cement to harden.

In our repair featured here, you will see that the peg holding the pearl on has broken off and is still in the hole of the pearl, so we need to remove it first.

You will not be able to drill it out as the metal is harder than the pearl. If you try to drill it out, the drill will likely move off the end of the peg and into the pearl, as it's softer.

Pearl ring with a fractured post stuck inside.

Carbide ball burr to remove post from pearl.

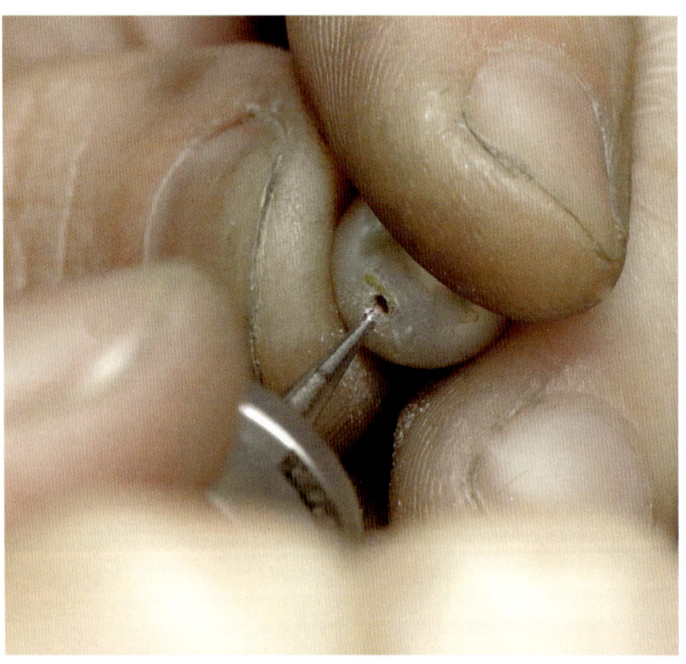

A burr is easier to direct than a drill.

HOLDING PEARLS AND BEADS

Having a pearl and bead clamp to hold the pearl in place whilst drilling or grinding will make holding the pearl easier.

Holding pearl in bead clamp to make post removal easier.

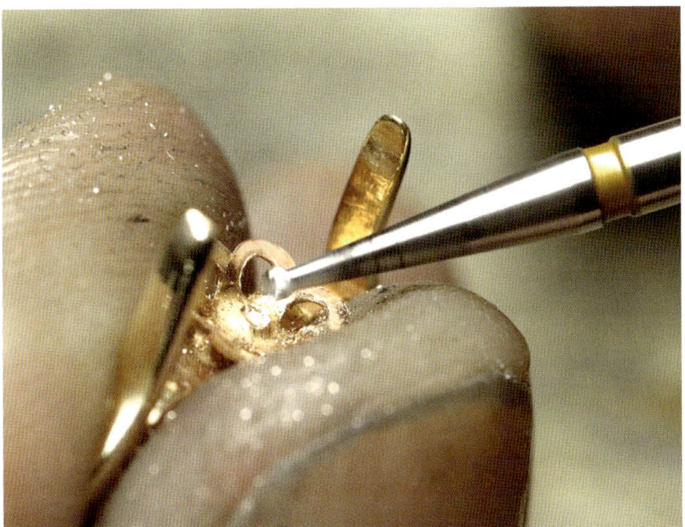

Removing the residual post and creating divot for new post.

Sweating solder onto end of new post.

New post successfully soldered to ring.

In this case I would tend to use a small carbide ball burr a few tenths of a millimetre smaller than the hole.

You will be able to direct the burr more easily than a drill, plus it will grind away the peg more easily than a drill. You will have to brace your hands to stop the drill from moving, to concentrate it solely on the metal peg.

If there is any of the old post still left in the pearl cup, then use a ball burr to grind it away and make a small divot where we are going to solder the new post.

Now we need to solder a new peg onto our item. Take some square section wire of the same material the item is made from. If the hole is 1mm in diameter then the wire needs to be 0.8mm square. Assess whether it is safe to solder a peg onto the item. If there are any gemstones or pearls etc that need protecting from the heat of the soldering, then protect them with a thermal paste. If there are any areas to be soldered immediately adjacent to something that could be damaged by heat, no amount of thermal paste will help. In this instance, it may be better to use a laser or pulse welder to attach the post as these pieces of equipment do not generate enough widespread heat to cause damage.

Sweat-solder a small pallion of the same metal and colour as the parent item onto the end of the wire.

Clean the immediate area where we are going to solder the post onto, adding flux to this and the soldered end of the peg. Gently heat the receiving area. As the heat increases then bring the wire peg towards the area, held in

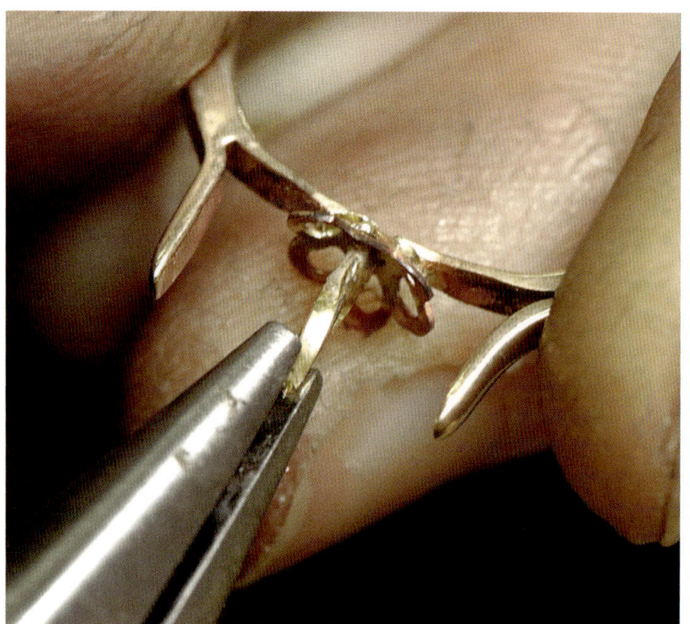

Twist post into a loose spiral.

Try the pearl in situ and adjust the post as necessary.

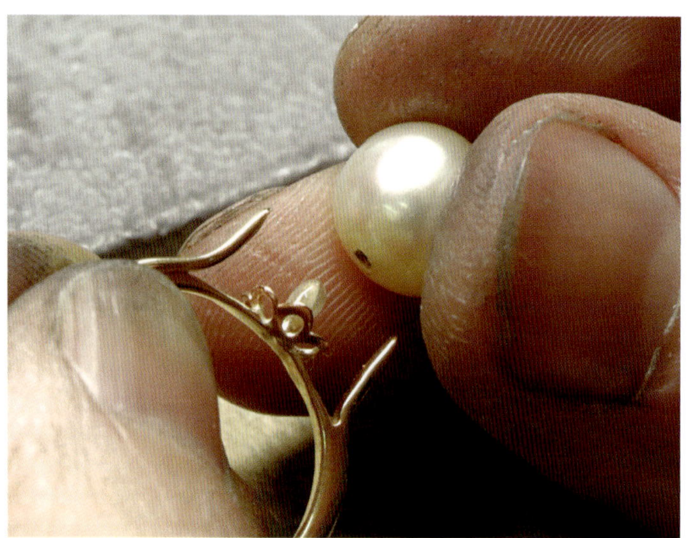

Cement pearl in place.

a pair of tweezers. Look at the colour change of the flux; this will be a good indication of when the area is the right temperature. As the area nears this temperature, bring the peg into contact, and the heat from the item will be transferred onto the peg.

When both parts are the right temperature, the solder will flow from the peg onto the item, forming a successful solder join. We solder this way because if we added the heat directly onto the wire before the rest of the item was at the correct temperature, there would be a chance the wire would melt, as it would heat up more quickly due to its size.

Once the item has cooled down, assess if it can be put in the safety pickle. Twist the wire into a loose spiral of approximately 5mm in length; make it slightly longer than the depth of the hole in the pearl. Clean the area with the necessary wheels and mops. Pre- and final polish the piece. Clean with warm soapy water or ultrasonic it if the item allows.

Put the pearl onto the new peg and see how far it comes down. Cut the peg to the necessary length and put the pearl back on the peg to make sure it goes down all the way, leaving no gap between the pearl and the item.

You can now cement in place. Add some pearl cement to the twisted peg and also into the pearl hole if possible, and twist the pearl onto the peg. Remove any excess cement with a cocktail stick or clean tissue. Leave for the required setting time.

When mixing up two-part epoxy resin, do so on a Post-it pad. Squeeze out equal amounts of hardener and resin. Even though you will be using a small amount for the final application, squeeze out more than you need; at least 10–20mm of each.

It's easier to ensure getting an equal amount on a bigger scale than on a smaller one. Mix well for a minute or so and use. After you have finished, simply tear off the top sheet of paper and throw away.

Two-part epoxy resin.

Squeeze out equal amounts.

Mix well.

CHAPTER 9

CLEANING, POLISHING AND RESTORING SURFACES AND TEXTURES

RESHAPING AND REFINISHING

If you already make jewellery, reshaping and refinishing scratched and worn jewellery should be second nature to you, but there are still a few problems we have to look out for.

If a ring comes in to you that is misshapen then you need to assess the severity. Is it simply out of shape or is the damage more serious? Perhaps the shank has detached itself from the head. In which case the item needs to be cleaned using an ultrasonic bath and preferably a steam cleaner before you tackle the repair.

If the ring is out of shape, then look at the inside of the shank to check for any hollowing of the shank and shoulders. You don't want to be hammering these areas when tapping it round. If there are hollow areas, mark the outside of the shank with a Sharpie to avoid those areas. Look at the setting. Are there any claws that need building up? Once the ring has been cleaned, stones can come out, as sometimes they are held in place with the dirt that has accumulated under the stone and within the setting. If this is the case, contact the client to explain that certain claws will need retipping due to wear.

Now we have assessed the ring we need to tap it round on a mandrel with a rawhide or plastic mallet, paying attention to any areas of hollowness inside the shank. I always hold my finger over the head of the ring to avoid shocking the stones whilst I am hammering, and I always wear an apron so if any stones happen to come loose then they will be caught in my apron and I do not have to spend hours on my hands and knees on the floor looking for that elusive stone.

Additionally, if the ring has any stones in the head, look to see if the cutlet (bottom) of the stone is protruding into the space where your finger goes. If it does, then you will need to use a grooved mandrel. The groove is there to allow the cutlet to protrude whilst still being able to tap the ring round.

Once the ring is nice and round it is time to remove any surface scratches. You may have to use a file to remove deep marks that a buff stick cannot remove. A ring file is a great time saver here, as you can use the same file on the outside and the inside without having to swap over. As you file, move to match the contour of the ring both inside and out. This is to ensure there are no flat spots introduced on the surface of the metal. Once you have removed all those deep marks, swap over to a buff stick.

I am pretty lazy here. I keep several buff sticks in one grit, usually 600-grit, but they are all in varying stages of wear, each with finer grits. So, start with a new buff stick or one that is rougher that all the others, and start buffing. If you buff the metal in a different direction to the filing, you will see when you have removed the previous file marks. Once all those file marks have been removed, swap over to a finer buff stick, again buffing in a slightly different direction, so you can see when you have removed all the previous coarse buff stick marks.

Rubber sanding wheels, silicon carbide wheels and white nylon brushes are the best for cleaning around settings and areas that buff sticks cannot reach. Rubber wheels and silicon carbide wheels are available in a variety of grits too, so start with a rough one and work towards the finer grit.

As well as all the silicone sanding drums available, round emery sticks can be used. Round dowels of wood wrapped

OPPOSITE: Polishing a ring.

Misshapen ring on a mandrel.

Reshaping ring using a rawhide mallet and mandrel.

Buffing the ring.

Silicon carbide wheel reaching areas a buff stick can't.

BUFFING PLATINUM

You will need to keep buff sticks to be used solely for platinum, as you must not contaminate the surface of platinum with other metal. This also applies to files and polishing mops.

Due to the nature of platinum and palladium, you'll have to buff the surface to a much finer grit. Here I would actually use specified grit emery paper, as you must buff to at least 2,000 - grit. The surface of platinum and palladium does not flow like silver and gold, so it has to be in the semi-shiny state just from the buff sticks, before starting to polish.

with a sheet of emery paper. These are very handy to have along with flat buff sticks but recently I have started to use sanding rolls in my flex shaft. These are available in grits 180 through to 2,000 and above. They are quicker to use than the round buff sticks.

Once you have produced a clean and smooth surface, it's time to start polishing. I always start with the inside of the ring. Once I have gone down to a sanding roll of approximately 800- to 1,000-grit, I swap over to a white nylon brush and run it through a pre-polish first. I like to

Sanding inside the ring using a sanding drum.

Polishing inside the ring, using a white nylon brush and tripoli.

Polishing outside the ring, using a bench-mounted polishing mop and tripoli.

Polished ring in an ultrasonic bath.

use tripoli polish. Spinning the brush at a medium speed, I angle it so it's not running along the shank in the direction of the previous sanding rolls I used. I do this so I can easily see if the nylon brush has cleaned up the metal – if it has, I will not be able to see the previous marks put in by the sanding roll. I charge up the nylon brush at regular intervals by running it against the tripoli polish. Not everyone can get used to these white nylon brushes, so hard felt mops are often used in the same way.

Once the inside of the shank is shiny, turn your attention to the outside. There are lots of mops to use in your flex shaft, but for speed and efficiency use a bench-mounted polishing motor. These mops rotate at approximately 3,000rpm and if you use the largest mops that will fit on the machine, usually 150mm (6 inch), you will be able to polish the outside quickly.

Start off with a calico mop and offer up some pre-polish or tripoli polish to the mop when it is rotating. Use the

When using a bench-mounted polishing motor, never put your fingers through the ring or bangle when you are polishing it. If the mops grab onto the item you are polishing, there may be a chance that your hand will be pulled with it. It is better to adopt an open grip, simply holding each side of the ring or bangle for instance. Then if the mop grabs the item from you, it will simply be pulled from your grip.

How not to use a bench-mounted polishing mop to polish a ring.

How to correctly use a bench-mounted polishing mop to polish a ring.

lower quarter of the mop when polishing and keep moving the ring back and forth, side to side, to wear the mop evenly across the surface. Every few moments, apply more polish. If you hold the item at an angle to the direction of the emery sticks used when buffing, you will be able to see when you have removed all the previous signs of buffing. Once you are happy with the finish, clean the item in an ultrasonic cleaner to remove all the polish and if you have a steamer, give it a blast with that too.

Back to the polishing motor and this time we want to use a soft swansdown mop with some final polish, I like to use rouge. Apply this in the same way as the pre-polish and polish the item to a superior high shine. Another immersion in the ultrasonic bath and steamer will remove the final polish from the piece.

Simply pat the item dry with a soft paper towel. You can buy drying equipment – round metal boxes called sawdust driers. Items to be dried are placed into boxwood sawdust, which is heated by a low element in the base of the container. The surface is left immaculate, with no water marks at all.

PLATING

Gold and rhodium plating in the workshop can be an expensive process to set up. In the larger workshop there is usually more space to cater for the multi-bath arrangements. There are smaller units available, which we have in our workshop. These take up very little worktop space, but even this can be a bit overkill for a small workshop.

This is where pen platers come in very handy. Pen platers are small units that are portable so they can be put away when not in use. Pen plating is a means of electroplating metal, such as gold and rhodium, onto specific areas of an item. It is as simple as using the fibre tip to paint the metal onto the piece of jewellery.

Often when jewellery is repaired, only a small area will need to be plated, such as a jump ring on a highly plated chain, or a couple of claws or tips that you have just repaired. This is where a pen plater comes in very handy, as you can simply apply the chosen metal colour to the selected area and not have to plate the whole item, saving money and time.

The advantages of pen plating are:

- Convenience – the unit is ready when you are. You do not have to wait for the plating baths to heat up.
- Precision – a fibre tip offers greater control than bath plating, only plating where it is needed. If you wanted to plate a specific area with the bath system, a stop off lacquer would need to be applied to the item and cleaned off afterwards.
- Cost effective – the cost of a pen plater is a lot less that purchasing large bath platers and the larger amount of solutions required.
- Ease of use – a simple small unit with a rotary control allows a change of voltage for different metal applications and a 'pen' to draw with.
- Materials – due to the small quantities of solution needed, there are various metal types available such as 18ct gold yellow, 18ct rose, white rhodium and black rhodium.
- Small workshop-friendly – pen plating is a safe and easy process that can be carried out on a small scale.

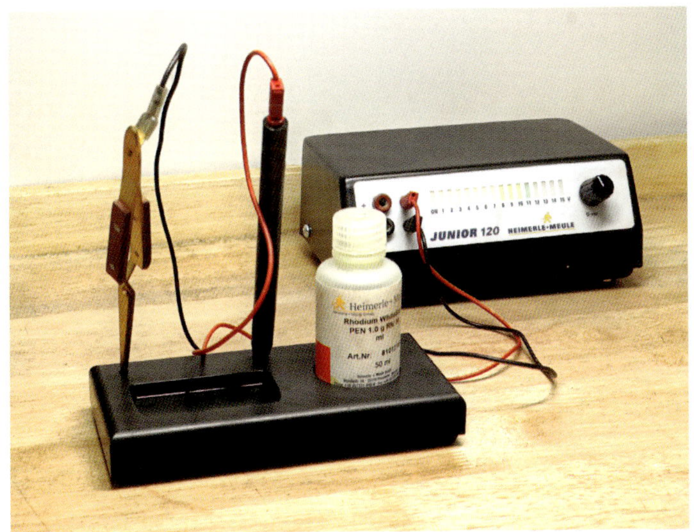

Pen plating setup.

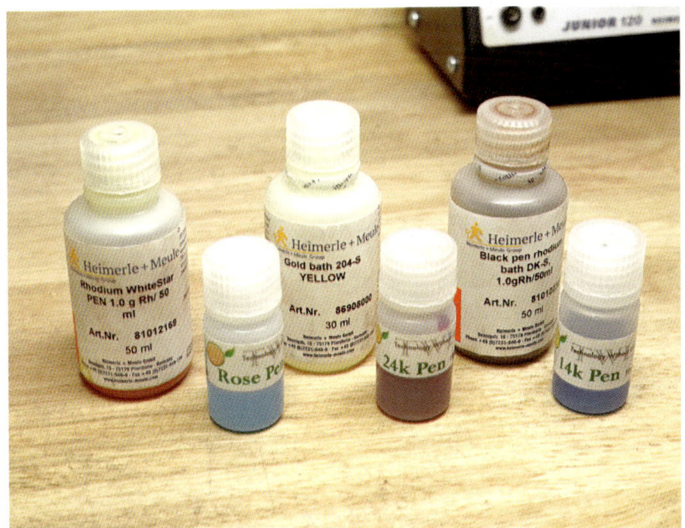

Assorted pen plating solutions.

How to Use Your Pen Plater to Selectively Plate Rhodium and Gold

To achieve an even and long-lasting result ensure that the item is absolutely free from dirt and grease. You can use an ultrasonic bath and/or steam cleaner.

Plug the tweezers and the plating pen into the unit, making sure you match up the colours black to black and red to red. Adjust the required voltage as is usually specified on the individual plating solution.

Use the tweezers to hold your item.

Dip the felt tip of the electroplating pen into your chosen plating solution.

Start coating the area to be plated by gently wiping across the surface. The felt tip must glide across the surface – without using any pressure!

Rinse your plated part thoroughly under running water and dry it carefully.

Rhodium Plating

It is important to remove all traces of the previous rhodium plating. This is achieved by using your buff sticks and emery paper.

Then we need to polish the item, getting into all the corners with brushes and mops, bringing the item to a high shine.

For the plating to take to the item, there must be no traces of grease or dirt. Use an ultrasonic bath and then a steam cleaner if you have one. From here on, do not touch the item with your fingers because even the grease from your fingers can inhibit the plating.

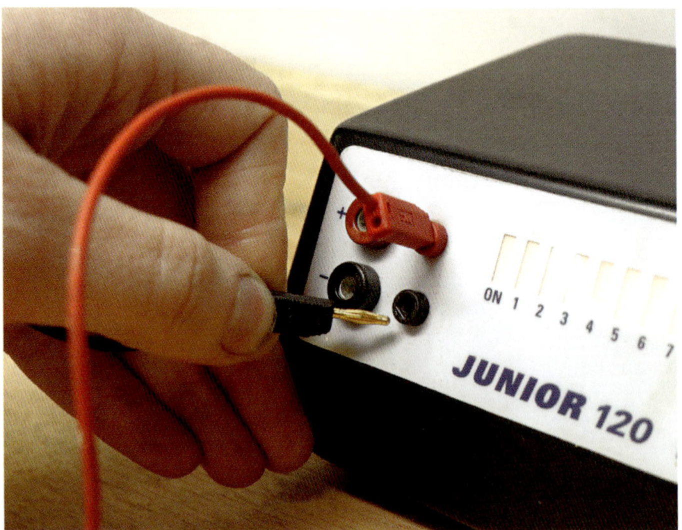

Plugging in tweezers and plating pen, ensuring colours are paired up.

Item to be plated securely in tweezers.

Collecting the plating solution.

Application of plating solution.

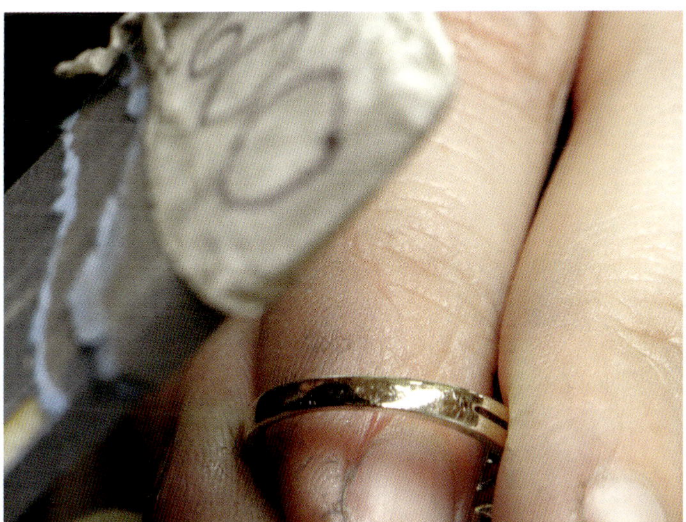

Removal of all previous traces of plating using buff stick.

Polishing the item.

Removal of all traces of grease and dirt.

Item in the plating bath.

The ring after plating.

Most white gold is rhodium plated to make the surface of the gold pure white. White gold has a slight yellow tint to it due to pure gold being yellow and alloyed with white metals. We must remove all traces of the old rhodium from the surface of white gold, otherwise when we come to re-rhodium the piece, the surface will have blemishes and the new rhodium layer will not be able to adhere to the surface properly.

Magic Rhodium.

Place the item on the rack and degrease it first. Next immerse it in a drag-out bath (a bath of plain distilled water) and then immerse it in the rhodium solution, gently agitating it.

After the required time in the rhodium bath, wash it in the next drag-out bath and then dry carefully, taking care not to scratch the beautiful white plating.

Using Magic Rhodium

If you only wish to rhodium plate small areas, such as claws that you may have retipped, there is a solution called Magic Rhodium. This solution is dangerous, and all PPE should be worn when using it (eye protection, a mask over the mouth and nose, and gloves).

This small bottle contains a white fluid that actually contains silver as a suspension, so no rhodium at all, which allows small areas to be repaired quickly without the use of electroplating equipment, and without the whole item being completely rhodium plated.

The surface to be 'rhodiumed' needs to be degreased and dried before Magic Rhodium is painted on with a small artist's brush.

The solution is allowed to dry on the surface and then buffed with a soft cloth to a high bright white shine.

Painting on the Magic Rhodium.

Buffing to a high shine.

REAPPLYING TEXTURES

A lot of the textures you come across on jewellery can easily be applied by hand. Over years of wear, the detail of texture can become eroded, especially with rings, and we can easily replicate this texture. Assessing the jewellery beforehand and taking steps to prevent any marks to the pattern or texture is essential. If you can protect the jewellery from damage when repairing it you won't need to reapply it, so always think ahead. For example, when sizing down a patterned or textured wedding ring, line the shrinking dies with some cloth to prevent the outside surface of the ring coming into contact with the dies and marking it. You should be able to shrink a ring this way by a couple of sizes. The inside of the ring may take on a slight 'orange peel' texture, but that can easily be cleaned up with a fine sanding drum and then polished.

Before we carry out any kind of repair we must assess the original texture: is it hammered, frosted, bark-like, polished or stippled? Is the texture uniform or directional? How deep is it? Often photographing the piece at this stage will help later.

We must try to preserve as much of the original texture as possible. It may not be possible to completely remove scratches off a ring shank, for example, if it would mean completely removing the original texture.

There are a few pieces of equipment you need to apply textures, such as glass fibre brush, a brass brush, used emery paper, texture wheels, mill grain or a set of beading tools and a polished square graver. These will replace original textures in most cases. So we need to choose the correct tool for the texture.

Hammered textures: Use the same style hammer (ball-peen, cross-peen, planishing hammer) with light, controlled blows. Work outward from the repaired section to blend.

Satin/Brushed: Use Scotch-Brite wheels, 3M radial bristle discs, or emery paper in the correct grit. Match the original grain direction.

Using a ball pen hammer to recreate a dimpled took.

Assortment of tools to recreate textures on jewellery.

Frosted or matte: Go for a fine abrasive wheel, frosting wheel, glass bristle brush, or fibre wheel. For very fine matte finishes, use a rubber wheel or even pumice powder.

Bark or organic textures: Needle files, burrs, or engraving tools can recreate irregular lines. Work slowly and vary depths for a natural appearance.

Milligram: Use a beading tool or sharp punch to tap small circles into the metal.

Never just retexture the repaired spot as this will highlight the repair. Instead fade the texture out into the surrounding area, varying the pressure and tool angle so there's no harsh transition. Once you are happy with the restoration, you may need to go over the area with a soft rouge mop and then ultrasonic the item.

Sometimes the whole item has been oxidised or has an aged patina. After retexturing, use Liver of Sulphur or Platinol, or whichever oxidiser would match the original piece. Take care to avoid any gemstones. Wipe back the high points to match the original finish.

Reapplying textures is all about observation and consistency. Take your time, replicate the original marks, and blend carefully. When done right, the repair disappears – and the jewellery looks exactly as the maker intended.

A beading tool is being used to shape small grains of metal.

A fibre-wheel is used to reapply a brushed finish.

A sharp graver is engraving fine detail.

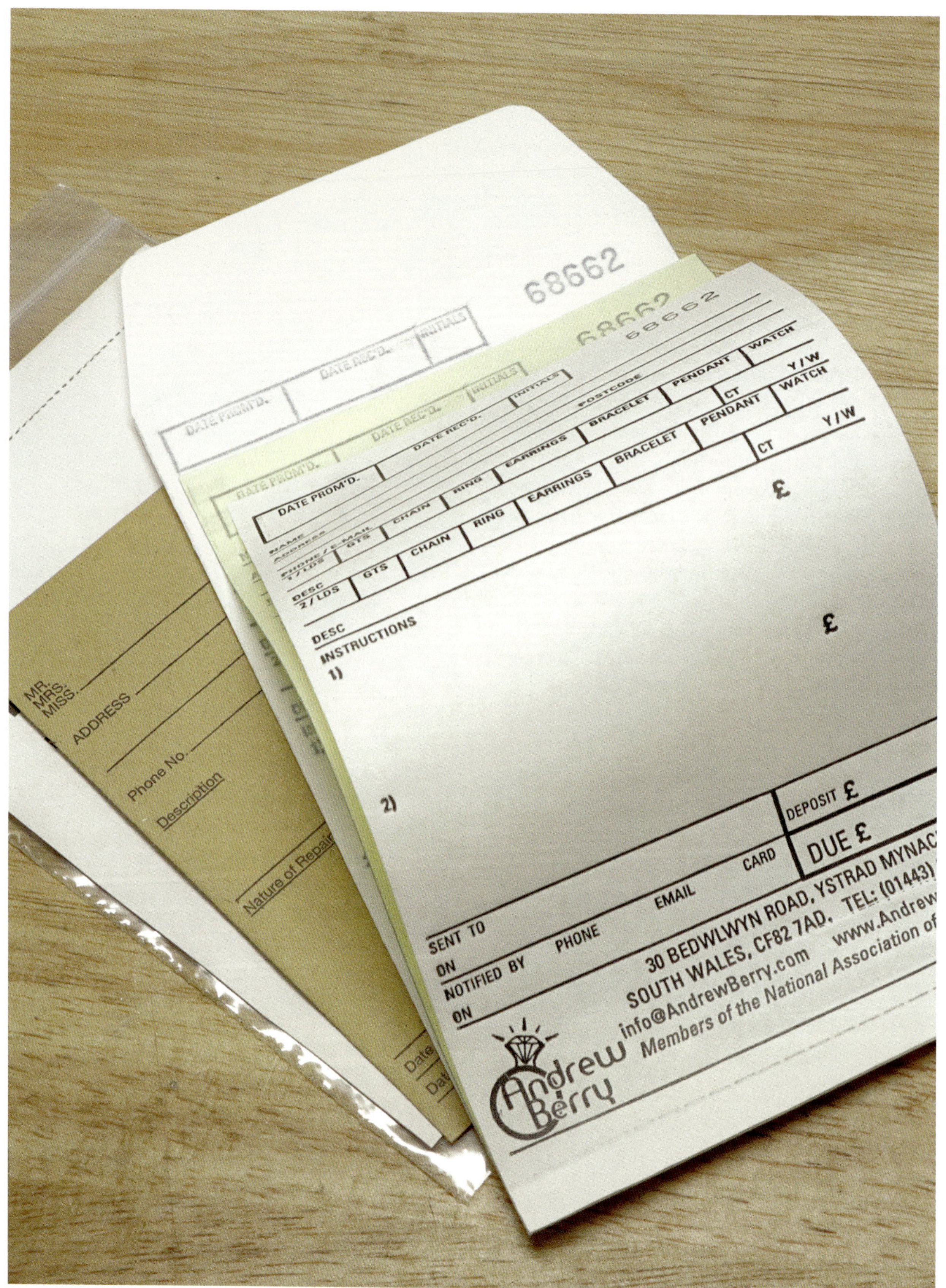
68662
68662
68662
DATE PROM'D.
DATE REC'D.
INITIALS
NAME
ADDRESS
PHONE / E-MAIL
POSTCODE
CHAIN
RING
EARRINGS
BRACELET
PENDANT
CT
WATCH
Y/W
GTS
DESC
17/LDS
£
2/LDS
DESC
£
INSTRUCTIONS
1)
2)
DEPOSIT £
CARD
DUE £
SENT TO
ON
EMAIL
PHONE
NOTIFIED BY
ON
30 BEDWLWYN ROAD, YSTRAD MYNACH
SOUTH WALES, CF82 7AD, TEL: (01443)
info@AndrewBerry.com   www.AndrewBerry.com
Members of the National Association of
Andrew
Berry
MR.
MRS.
MISS.
ADDRESS
Phone No.
Description
Nature of Repair
Date

TAKING IN AND COLLECTING REPAIRS

Take-in forms are important legal documents, evidencing custody and consent for the repair or modification. Effective record-taking protects both our client and ourselves. We need as much information as possible to be doing our best for our client. Information must be true, accurate, and with sufficient detail on the packet to empty all your jobs out, mix them up, and then be able to match them back up with the correct package (theoretically – we don't recommend doing this!).

Accurate descriptions of where a chain has broken, or which stone or claw has been replaced, is essential for a client's guarantee on the work – without this, it is virtually impossible to prove what future work is under guarantee and what is chargeable, meaning a potential awkward conversation with a client, or doing jobs free because it was impossible to prove otherwise.

If a client tries to rush the procedure, ask them to return when they have more time. The overwhelming majority of clients are reassured by the level of professionalism of a thorough take-in procedure.

Repair Packets

There are lots of types of commercial repair packet on the market, so pick whichever one suits your style and budget. The cheapest simply have a tear-off ticket number. We do not favour these, as the client really needs to have details of

WHAT DO WE NEED TO TAKE IN REPAIRS?

We know what tools we need to be able to repair jewellery, but we need additional equipment to be able to take in repairs.

The following, whilst not exhaustive, will help you be efficient:

- Repair envelopes or packets that you can write upon.
- Clear zip-lock small bags.
- Stone tweezers.
- Mandrel with ring sizes etched into it.
- A grooved mandrel with space to accommodate a ring where the stone is protruding into the finger space.
- Ring sizers. We have a few: narrow ones for narrow rings, medium width and wide gauges. You need to use a gauge that is the approximate width of the ring shank to get a true representation of the finger size.
- A ruler. We have one fastened onto our take-in counter. This enables you to measure the length of chains and also the position of the break in a chain.
- A 10× loupe is very important.
- A millimetre gauge. This could be a vernier or a dial type of gauge.
- An accurate scale capable of weighing to 1/10th of a gram.
- A diamond tester to help you distinguish between diamonds and their simulants. This is useful, but no substitute for close and careful examination under 10× loupe – after appropriate training your 10× loupe is your main tool for spotting diamond, moissanite and other simulants.
- Hand cream. This is to help the clients who force rings or the ring gauges on, and some tissues.

OPPOSITE: Repair packets.

the item they have left with you. Simply having a slip with a number on opens itself up to potential future problems. The client could state that they left several items with you, and you have no proof to say they did not.

Having an exact duplicate copy of the whole repair packet is the best option. You can buy triplicate repair packets with your name printed on; the top copy goes to the client, the second is for your records, and the third is usually the repair packet itself, which will include the details for the person carrying out the repair. If the third copy is not the packet then enclose this copy with the items in a clear bag.

Job reference numbers must be kept sequential – this ensures we are not missing any jobs. If a packet is spoilt, or a client changes their mind as you're writing it up, strike a line through and write 'error', 'client discarded', or 'client did not go ahead'. These records must be retained to keep sequential order, and a track on jobs.

Take-in forms and job packets are not to be left lying around. Great care must be taken while undertaking any photography in the workshop, to ensure customer details are not accidentally revealed on job packets or computer screens.

Examine the Item

Once you have the jewellery, examine it under magnification, such as with a 10× loupe. Check for missing, loose or chipped stones and bring these to your client's attention. It is best to do this before you clean the item. After all it would not be good to immediately start cleaning it and have a stone or two drop out. Mention that these stones may become dislodged when cleaned and advise on the best course of action.

Once the jewellery has been cleaned it's time to check it over closely. If there are any loose stones, then bring that to your client's attention. Show them and ask them if they want them tightened. Unless it's glaringly obvious, don't assume your client's issue is the problem you are seeing – always ask your client. Once you have determined the problem, have a think about all the necessary steps needed to complete the repair. If it is a ring, then are the stones

sensitive to heat? Can they be left in place and protected, or do they have to be taken out? If the ring is split or needs to be resized, is the ring shank too thin to make a satisfactory repair? Would it be better to replace part or the whole of the ring shank? These limitations will affect how you price the job.

Lockets usually contain photographs, but sometimes other things. We have seen ashes, hair and unidentified matter in lockets. Always ask your client to remove the contents, if possible, as heat may cause damage. If it can't be removed proceed with caution – consider whether you can use a torch, and don't even consider putting in an ultrasonic cleaner.

Filling out the Repair Packet

Record the date, the client's full details including postcode, telephone number and email address, and your initials as the person taking in the job. Ask if you can add them to your mailing list.

Record both initials – e.g. Andrew Berry will be AB. All personal details are confidential, and are not to be used or discussed outside of the workshop, or with any individual not in your employment.

Next, describe the item as best you can. Firstly, describe the metal (if applicable) – carat and colour. If there is no hallmark, record what is stamped on, but write 'stamped 375' instead of stating 9ct or 375 – the only guarantee of caratage is a UK hallmark. If there are no marks, simply state the colour of the metal, for example 'yellow-coloured metal'.

Say It with a Sketch

If you are not able to describe the item or the nature of the repair then a sketch is worth its weight in gold. Using a sketch can also reduce the amount of writing on the packet. A rough sketch of the setting showing which stone needs to be replaced or which claws need retipping makes it so much easier than trying to describe.

Make a note of any hallmark position to ensure the item is the right way around and avoid confusion at a later stage. Also make a note of any engraving on the item, including if it's on the inside of a ring shank. Sometimes if the engraving has been lasered on, it is not very deep and even polishing the ring could erase it. Make this known on the packet and also state this to the client. The same goes for some modern hallmarks. Manufacturers try to cut costs by having the hallmark lightly applied with a laser and sometimes you simply cannot avoid your polishing mops coming into contact with it. Whilst we do all we can to prevent polishing it away, sometimes the repair of the ring is so close to these marks that we simply cannot avoid it.

Items in a Packet

Try to keep the number of items in one packet to a minimum. We don't put more than two items in one packet, and the items must be wrapped to prevent abrasion damage. If more than one packet is used, number the packets 1 of 2, 2 of 2, and so on.

Promise a date that the repair is to be ready, and agree whether to call or email the client when it is ready for collection. Explain that if you need to buy in a stone or get a match on a gemstone, the repair may be slightly delayed. Keep your client up to date with the progress of the repair; even if there is no news, we always stay in touch so our client doesn't feel forgotten. If there is going to be an unexpected delay, then contact the client to say so.

Each time you contact the client, document it with the time and date and method of contact. Even if you have to leave a message, note that down too.

Chains and Bracelets

Name or describe the type of chain. If this isn't possible, and there is no one available to assist, a drawing will help – it needn't be artistic just a representation of the item. We carry a catalogue of chains and their names, for our team to refer to.

In the case of a fracture, always measure and record the full length, including where the fracture is – measure from the end and don't forget to note whether you've measured from bolt or jump end. When a chain gets pulled enough to snap, it's likely been stretched and is weaker afterwards, meaning it's more prone to break. People often assume it's

broken in the same place so it's vital to record exactly where the breakage is. This will help should the chain break again, and you will be able to see if the chain has broken in the same place (a no-charge repair) or in a different place (a chargeable repair). Take in any pendants that are worn on the chains in case the pendant bail or jump doesn't fit over the chain end after repair.

For storage, insert the chain into a zip-lock bag, keeping the clasp outside the bag, and zip it closed. When you remove the chain, simply hold the clasp and lift the chain out of the bag. This way will stop the chain from tangling in the packet.

You may be able to upsell when taking in chains. Take a close look at the wear on the clasp, the chain ends, the bail on a pendant. The chain may come in for a simple repair, but there are a few components that also tend to wear and it is better to replace or build them up now rather than end up losing the chain should they break or wear out at a later date.

The popularity of bracelets with charms comes and goes, but they are always a staple repair item. When taking in a charm bracelet it is important to count the number of charms along with a brief description of each, listing them in order. Depending on the type of repair, you may need to see if any of the jump rings attaching the charms are soldered. If the client wants a new charm added and soldered, take a look at all the other charms; you could make a bit of extra money by suggesting any unsoldered jump rings could be soldered. If they decline, say so on the packet.

Resizing Rings

Describe the design of the ring, for example motif style, cluster, solitaire, eternity, wedding band, and so on. It is a good idea to have diagrams of a wide range of styles to hand – again we have a catalogue of examples to refer to. When description has been exhausted, move on to stones. Include the type of setting, for example bezel-set, claw-set, flush-set.

Do not simply write 'increase/decrease by X number of sizes', or 'make a size X', this is insufficient. If the ring does not fit after resizing, a record of the original, and target size is needed. Note which finger has been measured and also on which hand. If a client supplies the target size, instead of you measuring the finger this needs to be noted – if the size is incorrect the additional workshop costs to redo are incurred by the client. Also note if the ring is to be stretched or a piece put in. If stretched, mention to your client that the shank may appear slightly thinner.

Start off by measuring your client's ring, sliding it down your ring mandrel. Check the ring is in contact with the mandrel all the way round and then read the size. If it is a narrow ring, read off where the leading edge of the shank is, but if the ring is any wider, then judge the middle of the back of the ring shank and see where this lies on the mandrel. If the bottom of the stone sits below into the finger hole, then use the grooved mandrel so you do not damage the stone.

Now we have assessed the ring size, we need to find out the size of the client's finger. Having several width gauges for your client to try on is the most accurate way to ensure finger measurements. Use the narrow gauges for narrow rings and wide gauges for wide rings. Ask your client to try a ring gauge on that is a couple of sizes larger than the ring measured. If you can clearly see that the ring gauge will not fit, select a gauge a couple of sizes bigger again. It is better to be too big and work smaller than start too small. The client will not be tempted to force on the sizer, causing problems trying to remove it from the finger. No one wants a ring gauge stuck on their finger.

When deciding on a shank repair, take into consideration the width and thickness of the shank. If the shank is thin, suggest a 1/4 or 1/2 shank. State the width and thickness of the shank when the ring is taken in, so there will be no confusion later on at collection.

What is the best fit?
Some people like their rings tight, others want a looser fit if their fingers swell slightly, but the ideal fit is where the gauge slides over the knuckle comfortably with a slight resistance. Usually when the gauge is removed, there is more resistance coming over the knuckle due to the gauge pulling on the skin on that part of the finger. When trying on wide gauges this is extremely important.

When the gauge is on the finger it may feel loose and the client may want the ring tighter, but the important size is the knuckle. If the client wants the ring any tighter then there may be a chance that the ring gauge will not come off, this is where the hand lotion comes handy to help with gauges that become a little hard to remove.

Can the ring be stretched or does it need a piece put in? Again, write this information out on the packet so if another jeweller were to size the ring, they know exactly what needs to be done.

If the ring shank is cracked or split then you will still need to record the original size of the ring. If the client asks for it to be soldered, they may come back saying the ring is now smaller than it was before and you would then have to resize the ring free of charge because there is no evidence of the original size.

If at any stage the client does not agree with your suggested repair, such as wanting a different ring size to the one you suggest, or if you suggest a 1/4 or 1/2 shank and they decline and simply want the shank resoldered, then always write this on the packet. State that the repair was suggested but the client declined. This is to prevent any further problems should the ring not fit correctly, or the ring shank splits soon after. State to the client that if we undertake the repair based upon what they want and it turns out to be incorrect or the repair does not last, you will have to charge them again to redo the repair.

Stones

It is not our job to presume or identify a stone, or even to take our client's word for it. Say what you see. Describe as accurately as you can, sticking to the facts that are plain. Record colour, shape, size, transparency, and cut (for example faceted or cabochon). Check for any laser inscriptions on stone girdles and record if present. What are the pitfalls of mis-describing something? 'You acknowledged my stone, that you took in, was a diamond – you wrote it on the report. What I got back was not a diamond therefore you switched my stone.' The financial implications of this are huge, and may be recoverable, but the cost to your image and perceived integrity may not be.

Is the stone missing completely or has the client retrieved it? Don't leave anything to interpretation. Which stone(s) are we talking about? How are you going to locate them? The easiest and clearest way to interpret this is to draw a picture. If a stone is symmetrical, don't forget to include the side/orientation of the hallmark or stamp, otherwise the piece could be inverted and we're back to square one. Notate claws and tips also – considering orientation. Advise that replaced claws will appear slightly bulkier than worn ones; the client may decide to replace all claws. Record the fact you gave them this advice.

Beads

Count the beads, instead of measuring the length of the necklace – the silk or cord may be stretched – and explain that the necklace may be shorter after restringing. Measure the diameter of the beads, and if they are graduated, measure the largest, and the smallest.

Additional Observations

Reporting general condition and future risks is an important conversation to have at the time of take-in, rather than later when the job is collected. Reporting on general condition, for example abrasions to metal or gemstones, cracks or fissures, missing stones, and so on, is essential as evidence of condition at the time the item came into our care – even if the client does not want to go ahead with rectifying this.

Make a note that the condition and risks were discussed, and what the outcome was – did the client go ahead or decline? Don't be afraid of offering more, for example a new half-shank on a worn ring that is being resized may be a better option, giving the piece greater longevity – record the choice given by the client. There may well be missing stones that the client hasn't noticed – even if they decide to do nothing about this, it needs to be recorded as an observation.

Photographs are worth their weight in gold as backup while items are entrusted to your care – both at take-in and after the repair is complete. After all your assessments, sometimes, jewellery is irreparable, but you can have a conversation about a new commission if your client wants to retain that sentimentality.

Disclaimers

Risks should be discussed and recorded – for example the possibility of stones becoming dislodged during ultrasonic cleaning, and the charges incurred to replace them. Clients commonly ask for all stones to be checked – we are unable to offer guarantees on stones and settings, as accidental damage can occur at any time. All that can be assured is that the stones were secure on the day they were checked. Occasionally, jobs are undertaken against our advice; these are always 'at customer's risk' and it is vital that this is recorded. We reserve the right to decline a job deemed too risky, and this is always preferable to undertaking work at the customer's risk.

Dealing with the Repair Packets

So now you have accepted several repairs, how you go about the next stage can influence your client's perception of you. This next stage is dependent on how many repairs you take in, but start as you mean to go on, and as you build up your repair business it will become second nature.

At the end of each day take a look through the repairs that have been taken in with the following considerations:

- Does the description on the packet accurately reflect the contents?
- Check if you have the necessary findings to complete the jobs in hand.
- Do you have all the metal needed to complete the sizing or reshanking jobs? If you have to order materials, are you able to order them in low quantities with low carriage costs, or is it better to wait a few days to order larger quantities at a lower price with one carriage cost? This would depend on the collection date of the repair. If you have to order supplies for a job, then write the date ordered on the packet. We have space for this on our repair packets.
- If you have the findings and/or metal in stock, put them in the relevant repair packets so you have an idea of what needs to be ordered in time for the next repair.
- If you have repair packets with separate duplicate or triplicate pages, separate the slips so you always have a copy on hand that you can refer to, should the item become damaged or even lost.
- If you have a few jewellers carrying out the repairs, delegate who gets what and put their initials on the packet. This helps if there is a problem with the repair, as you know who to approach for help.

While-You-Wait Repairs

We do not favour a while-you-wait service, as this can often result in you rushing a repair, plus you still have to carry out the take-in procedures just in case anything should happen. Some repairs can be carried out quickly, within minutes, and by charging the same or even more for the while-you-wait service, the client sees exactly how long a repair can take without even taking into consideration the years you have taken to learn the craft or the cost of the equipment being used. All they see is the time it's taken and the cost they are being charged. It's better to take a bit longer on while-you-wait repairs, just so the extra time you take adds value to the repair.

Don't Take in Boxes

Politely request your clients to keep their boxes. Boxes do not always fit inside the repair packets, and it is inconvenient to have to remember to give them back – plus they take up a lot of room. Place the item in the packet and hand the boxes back, stating that their item is better stored in the packet in the safe.

Valuations

The one question we are asked virtually on a daily basis, is 'What is my item worth?' This question alone is never enough to provide an answer, as many additional factors need to be established to even arrive at a starting point to determine 'worth' or value. This always prompts a conversation about levels of valuation, and the most important question – for what purpose does the client want the information; what do they intend to do with the information, and the item as a result? An insurance valuation, for the purposes of replacement with a new item in the event of loss, will look very different to an open market valuation – an estimation of what they could realise should they sell the item at auction.

A jewellery valuation is a researched, expert opinion, so quoting what you could charge to replace an item, does not constitute a valuation, this is merely a quote to replace.

Registered jewellery valuers are highly trained specialists, with appropriate gemmology training and qualifications. We would recommend referral to a National Association of Jewellers Institute Registered Valuer for a client enquiring about valuation. The National Association of Jewellers can also advise on the training required to embark on the registration pathway.

COLLECTING REPAIRS

It is important to have a system for managing the collection or return of repairs, primarily to keep track of the items in your possession, but also to ensure that you are paid for your work in a timely manner.

When items are collected from our store, we ask our clients to return the triplicate receipt provided at take-in. This way, we know the item has been collected. Occasionally people lose this, in which case we ask for photo ID and ask them to sign a document to acknowledge receipt of the item. Whatever the system, it must be robust and fully understood by everyone involved in every stage of the process.

Depending on the nature of the repair, and our present workload, we tend to advise a turnaround time of two to three weeks. We always specify a time frame, and most often, the job is ready to collect before the specified date – in which case it's always nice to telephone your client and exceed their expectation. Staying in touch builds your relationship and trust, while keeping your revenue stream flowing. Similarly, it is important to stay in touch with your client if it's looking like the job may take longer than expected to complete.

Unclaimed Repairs: How to Handle Them

Very occasionally, a client may fail to collect their jewellery. The National Association of Jewellers in the UK has a Code of Practice that will help you should this ever happen. Your country may have its own rules and regulations.

For most jewellery retailers, uncollected repairs aren't a major issue – but they're still an inconvenience. To prevent this from becoming a recurring problem, always take complete contact details when accepting items for repair. This includes the customer's full name, address, email, and phone number. If they have a backup contact method, make sure to take that down too.

Generally, giving a customer up to six months to retrieve their repaired item is considered fair. But you are entitled to send a formal notice (explained below) any time after the repair is completed, as long as the agreement whether it is

Client
collecting repairs.

spoken or written, was that the item would be picked up once it was ready.

Including a clear statement on your repair receipt can be an effective deterrent. For example: 'Please collect your repaired item within six months of notification. Items left beyond this period may be disposed of.'

If the Item Isn't Collected — What Are Your Rights?

If a customer doesn't return for their item, you're able to recover your costs by following the proper legal process outlined in the Torts (Interference with Goods) Act 1977, which grants you, the bailee, a right to sell the item under specific conditions. *See* the Appendix for a sample letter. Here's how to proceed:

Step 1: Issue a notice

The first step is to formally notify the customer, obligating them to collect their goods. You should already have a general notice visible in-store (and ideally also printed on receipts), stating how long you'll keep items before taking further action. If not, or if extra steps are required, you'll need to send a written notice via hand delivery, or Recorded or Special Delivery to your customer's known address. This notice should include:

1. The customer's name and address
2. A detailed description of the item, and where it is being stored
3. Confirmation that the repair is complete
4. Any outstanding charges owed before the notice was issued.

Step 2: Send a notice of intent to sell

If the customer still hasn't collected their item after a reasonable period (usually 2–4 weeks), you can move to the next stage by issuing a 'Notice of Intent to Sell'. This written notice (again sent via recorded or special delivery) must contain:

1. The customer's name and address
2. A clear description of the item and its location
3. The proposed date of sale
4. Details of any amount you plan to retain from the sale – covering the repair and other legitimate expenses
5. A timeframe that gives the customer a fair chance to retrieve the item before the sale
6. If money is still owed for the repair, the customer must be given at least three months from the notice date to collect their goods.

A few important legal reminders

- You cannot proceed with a sale if there is an unresolved dispute over payment or the repair itself.
- If you can't contact the customer, you must show that you made reasonable efforts to do so. This might include posting a notice in your shop window, on your website or social media, or even publishing an ad in a local newspaper for at least three months.
- After selling the item, you may deduct the repair cost and any reasonable selling expenses (like advertising). Any remaining money must be held for six years, in case the customer returns to claim it.

You meet the legal standard in the UK if your store displays a clear notice stating that repaired goods will be held for six months and may be disposed of afterward. To reinforce this, include the same policy on customer receipts.

APPENDIX

RING SIZES

UK, Australia, New Zealand	USA, Canada	India, China, Japan	Europe	Inside Diameter (mm)	Inside Circumference (mm)
A	1/2		38	12.04	38
A1/2	3/4			12.24	38.5
B	1	1	39	12.45	39
B1/2	1 1/4			12.65	39.7
C	1 1/2		40.5	12.85	40.4
C1/2	1 3/4			13.06	41
D	2	2	42.5	13.25	41.6
D1/2	2 1/4			13.46	42.3
E	2 1/2	3	43	13.67	43
E1/2	2 3/4			13.87	43.6
F	3	4	44	14.07	44.2
F1/2	3 1/4	5		14.27	44.8
G	3 1/2		45	14.48	45.5
G1/2	3 3/4	6		14.68	46.2
H	4	7	46.5	14.88	46.8
H1/2	4 1/4			15.09	47.4
I	4 1/2	8	48	15.29	48
I1/2				15.39	48.4
J	4 3/4		49	15.49	48.7
J1/2	5	9		15.70	49
K	5 1/4		50	15.9	50
K1/2	5 1/2	10		16.1	50.5
L	5 3/4		51.5	16.31	51.5
L1/2	6	11		16.51	51.9

UK, Australia, New Zealand	USA, Canada	India, China, Japan	Europe	Inside Diameter (mm)	Inside Circumference (mm)
M	6 1/4	12	53	16.71	52.5
M1/2	6 1/2	13		16.92	52.8
N	6 3/4		54	17.12	53.4
N1/2	7	14		17.32	54
O	7 1/4		55	17.53	54.9
O1/2	7 1/2	15		17.73	55.7
P	7 3/4		56.5	17.93	56.2
P1/2	8	16		18.14	56.6
Q	8 1/4		58	18.34	57.5
Q1/2	8 1/2	17		18.53	58.2
R	8 3/4		59	18.75	58.9
R1/2	9	18		18.95	59.1
S	9 1/4		60	19.15	60.02
S1/2	9 1/2	19		19.41	60.6
T	9 3/4		61	19.56	61.4
T1/2	10	20		19.76	62.1
U	10 1/4	21	62.5	19.96	62.7
U1/2	10 1/2	22		20.17	63.4
V	10 3/4		64	20.37	64
V1/2	11	23		20.57	64.3
W	11 1/4		65	20.78	65.3
W1/2	11 1/2	24		20.98	65.7
X	11 3/4		66	21.18	66.6
X1/2	12	25		21.39	67.2
Y	12 1/4		68	21.59	67.8
Y1/2					
Z	12 1/2	26	69	21.89	68.5
Z 1/2	12 3/4			22	69.1
Z+1	13 1/4		70	22.4	70.4
Z+2	13 3/4			22.81	71.7
Z+3	14		72	23.01	72.3
Z+4	14 1/2			23.42	73.6
Z+5				23.82	74.1
Z+6				24.12	74.8

The measurement needed to remove or add one size to a ring is approximately:

UK, Australia and New Zealand – 1.5mm

USA and Canada – 2.5mm

Europe – 1.2mm

The actual size depends on the width and thickness of the ring shank.

Once you have had experience in sizing rings, you will be able to judge the exact amount to add or remove.

MOHS SCALE OF HARDNESS

Gemstone	Hardness
Agate	7
Alexandrite	8.5
Amber	2.5
Amethyst	7
Ametrine	7
Apatite	5
Aquamarine	7.5
Aventurine	7
Beryl	7.5
Bloodstone	7
Carnelian	7
Chalcedony	7
Citrine	7
Cubic zirconia	8.5
Diamond	10
Emerald	7.5
Fluorite	4
Garnet	6.5
Iolite	7
Jade	6
Jasper	7
Jet	2.5
Labradorite	6
Lapis lazuli	5.5
Malachite	4
Moonstone	6
Morganite	7.5
Obsidian	5
Onyx	7
Opal	6
Pearl	3
Peridot	6.5
Quartz	7

Ruby	9
Sapphire	9
Spinel	8
Talc	1
Tanzanite	6.5
Tiger's eye	7
Topaz	8
Tourmaline	7.5
Tsavorite	6.5
Turquoise	5
Zircon	7.5

Facetted Gemstone Terminology

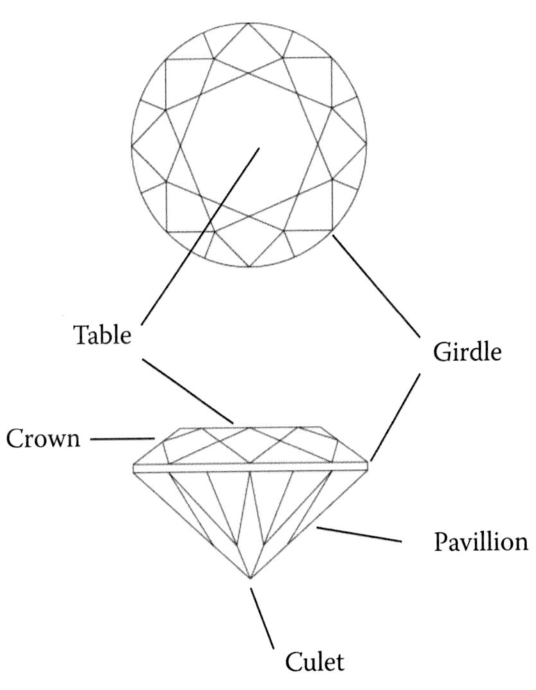

METAL THICKNESS CONVERSION

Brown & Sharpe (B&S) Gauge	Millimetres
0	8.5
1	7.3
2	6.5
3	5.8
4	5.2
5	4.6
6	4.1
7	3.6
8	3.2
9	2.9
10	2.6
11	2.3
12	2.1
13	1.8
14	1.6
15	1.45
16	1.3
17	1.14
18	1
19	0.9
20	0.8
21	0.7
22	0.6
23	0.55
24	0.5
25	0.45
26	0.4
27	0.35
28	0.3
29	0.27
30	0.25

GEMSTONE VULNERABILITY TABLE

Gemstone	Heat	Ultrasonic	Steam	Pickle	Polish
Alexandrite	X	X if fractured	X if fractured	X if fractured	✔ (depending on compound)
Amber	X	X	X	X	X
Aquamarine	X	✔	✔	✔ (but no hot pickle)	✔
Coral	X	X	X	X	X
Corundum (ruby and sapphire)	✔	✔	✔	✔	✔
Diamond	✔	✔	✔	✔	✔ (depending on compound)
Emerald	X	X	X	X	X
Garnet	X	✔ (except hydrogrossular/ demantoid – avoid)	X	X	✔ (depending on compound) avoid hydrogrossular
Glass	X	✔ (except moldavite)	X	X	X
Hematite	X	X	X	X	X
Howlite	X	X	X	X	X
Iolite	X	X	X	X	X
Jadeite	X	X	X	X	X
Jet	X	X	X	X	X
Labradorite	X	X	X	X	X
Lapis lazuli / sodalite	X	X	X	X	X
Malachite	X	X	X	X	X
Marcasite	X	X	X	X	X
Moissanite	✔	✔	✔	✔	✔ (depending on compound)
Moonstone	X	X	X	X	X
Nephrite	X	X	X	X	X
Opal	X	X	X	X	X
Pearl	X	X	X	X	X
Peridot	X	✔	X	X	X
Rock crystal	X	✔	✔	✔	✔ (depending on compound)
Quartz (agates, carnelian, chalcedony, onyx, jasper, aventurine)	X	X	X	X	X
Quartz (amethyst, ametrine, citrine)	X	✔	✔	✔	✔ (depending on compound)
Rhodochrosite	X	X	X	X	X
Shell	X	X	X	X	x
Spinel	✔	✔	✔	✔	✔ (depending on compound)
Topaz	X	X	X	X	X
Tourmaline	X	X	X	X	X
Turquoise	X	X	X	X	X
Zircon	X	X	X	X	X
Zoisite (tanzanite)	X	X	X	X	X

Notes:
Avoid 'thermal shock' for all stones.
Avoid ultrasonic and steam cleaning for all fractured, fracture-filled, chatoyant/star stones or heavily included stones.
A thermal protective gel is always recommended for covering gemstones when using a torch nearby, (including diamond and corundum).

TORTS (INTERFERENCE WITH GOODS) ACT 1977

This is an example letter that we send to clients who have not collected their items within a specified time frame. We print this letter out on headed paper and fill in the client's details and item's descriptions. This letter is in line with the National Association of Jewellers Code of Practice: Uncollected Items.

The following notice text needs to be easily visibly displayed inside the store:

Torts (Interference with Goods) Act 1977

Items left with us for repair will be kept for a minimum of 6 months after the repair is completed. Whilst we will try to contact you during this period to remind you to collect your goods, customers are advised that items that remain uncollected after this period will be disposed of.

Once disposed of we will deduct our reasonable costs and then attempt to contact you to return the balance.

This is a notice that needs to be easily visibly displayed in the store window, on your website or on social media. The intention here is to provide enough information to prompt someone's memory, without giving away any personal information:

Torts (Interference with Goods) Act 1977

A (brief description of article, for example 'ladies' watch') was left with us for repair by (Mr X) from (name of town) on (insert full date). We are still waiting for this item to be collected. Please be advised that if this item remains unclaimed by (a date 3 months from now) we will be disposing of the product.

LETTER HEADING GOES HERE

Date

NOTICE OF INTENTION TO SELL GOODS
Pursuant to Torts (Interference with Goods) Act,1977 Sec 12 (3)

For immediate attention of:
Name
....

Address
....

You left goods at:
(Name and address of business)
....
....
on (date)
....

The goods left are listed as:
....
....

This is in contravention of our terms and conditions.

NOTICE is hereby given that:

1. The author of this notice is the Involuntary Bailee of the goods referred to above.
2. The goods listed above must be collected within the next three months, the sum owing with regards to these goods is:
....
3. If you fail to arrange to collect the goods within the next three months, commencing with the date of this notice, the bailee intends to sell or otherwise dispose of the goods after that date. The costs of any sale or disposal will be deducted from any sum accrued and the remainder will be retained for a period of 6 years for you to claim.

Date: ....   Signed: ....

SUPPLIERS

ORGANISATIONS

UK
National Association of Jewellers
Tel: 01212 371110
Web: https://www.naj.co.uk
Email: membership@naj.co.uk

USA
Jewelers Of America
Tel: 800 223 0673
Web: https://www.jewelers.org
Email: members@jewelers.org

Canada
Canadian Jewellers Association
Tel: 416 368 7616
Web: https://canadianjewellers.com
Email: info@canadianjewellers.com

Stone Suppliers
A E Ward & Son
1ˢᵗ Floor, 86 Hatton Garden, London EC1N 8QQ
Tel: 02072 534036

UK Tool Suppliers
At The Bench Store
Tel: 01443 815555
Web: https://www.atthebench.store
Email: support@andrewberry.com

Cookson Gold
Tel: 03451 001122
Web: https://www.cooksongold.com
Email: info@cooksongold.com

Betts Metal Sales
Tel: 01212 332413
Web: https://www.bettsmetalsales.com
Email: sales@bettsmetals.co.uk

Durston Tools
Tel: 01494 342069
Web: https://www.durston.com
Email: support@durston.com

H S Walsh & Sons
Tel: 01959 543660
Web https://www.hswalsh.com
Email: mail@hswalsh.com

Armitage Tools
Web: https://www.armitagetools.co.uk
Email: admin@armitageonlineltd.co.uk

Maddisons of Durham
Tel: 01642 058107
Web: https://maddisonsofdurham.co.uk
Email: info@maddisonsofdurham.co.uk

Palmer Metals
Tel: 02476920163
Web: https://palmermetals.co.uk/
Email: sales@palmermetals.co.uk

USA Tool Suppliers
Rio Grande
Tel: 800 545 6566
Web: https://www.riogrande.com
Email: cscjewelrytech@riogrande.com

Gesswein
Tel: 203 366 5400
Web: https://www.gesswein.com
Email: info@gesswein.com

Stuller
Tel: 800 877 7777
Web: https://www.stuller.com/
Email: info@stuller.com

SEP Jewelry Tools of Chicago
Tel: 312 541 4554
Web: https://septools.com
Email: septools@septools.com

Otto Frei
Tel: 800 772 3456
Web: https://www.ottofrei.com
Email: info@ottofrei.com

Hoover & Strong
Tel: 800 759 9997
Web: https://www.hooverandstrong.com
Email: info@hooverandstrong.com

GRS Tools
Tel: 800 835 3519
Web: https://grs.com
Email: hello@grs.com

Hong Kong
Wing Wo Hong
Tel: (852) 2544 7932
Web: https://wingwohong.com
Email: info@wingwohong.com

GLOSSARY

Adhesive
A natural or man-made material that has sand-like qualities used to clean or remove marks on the surface. Often used on emery paper or wet and dry paper.

Anneal
To heat a piece of metal to restore its **malleability**.

Ball pein hammer
A hammer with one end shaped like a small ball. Used for shaping or texturing metal.

Base metal
A metal that does not have any precious metals in it. Brass, copper, steel, pewter and titanium are often called base metals.

Bench block
A small thick piece of flattened steel plate that is used to hammer metal on usually to make it straight.

Bench peg/pin
A wooden support that is attached to a jeweller's bench by vice or permanent fitting, to act as a support for filing or piercing.

Bevel
A slant or chamfer on a piece of jewellery.

Bezel
A rim of metal that sits around the circumference of a stone to secure it in place. Used in a rubover setting.

Burnish
The action relating to rubbing a hard object such as agate or steel against metal to polish and smooth the surface.

Burr
Small steel rods of different shapes and sizes that fit into a rotary tool used for grinding or shaping material.

Cabochon
A gemstone that has been cut and polished with a rounded, smooth top. Usually has a flat bottom.

Carat
A measure used to express the weight of a gemstone or diamond and also to express the purity of gold, with 24 carat being the purest.

Charcoal block
A small rectangular block of carbon used for soldering on.

Clasp
A way of joining a chain, necklace or bracelet securely, while allowing it to be removed.

Claw

The name given to a piece of metal that holds a stone into a setting. Also called a **prong**.

Crown

The top part of a faceted gemstone, leading from the table down to the girdle.

Culet

The very tip of a cut gemstone – the pointy end, if you will – is known as the culet.

Dividers

A tool that has two arms joined at one end, used for measuring or marking out.

Facet

A term relating to the cuts on a gemstone that form small polished flat surfaces.

Findings

A general term given to the small fittings for jewellery that are often commercially made.

Flux

A term given to a chemical that is applied to the surface of metal that aids soldering by cleaning the area of oxides.

Gauge

A measurement used to determine the thickness or diameter of metal.

Hallmark

A method of marking metal by one of the four UK Assay offices, comprising the maker's mark, the purity of metal, where it was stamped and the date it was stamped – although the date is an optional mark.

Hammer

A tool used for hitting or forming metal.

Inclusions

Inclusions are small foreign objects or minerals that have been trapped inside a gemstone while forming. Far from being a bad thing, they can give each gemstone a unique appearance. We often call them the fingerprints of Mother Nature.

Jump ring

A small round ring connecting components of a piece.

Lemel

The filings and dust created from filing or piercing off precious metals.

Malleability

The state of a piece of metal in its dead state – where it has no spring in it and is easily formed.

Mallet

Used to describe a non-metallic hammer.

Mandrel

Usually a tapered steel rod used for forming metal on.

Mop

A round material used for polishing.

Pallion/paillon

Small pieces of solder cut from a larger piece of solder.

Patina

A finish that appears on a metal surface as a result of exposing it to chemicals or a natural exposure to the air.

Pavillion

The pavillion is the part of the gemstone that stretches from the girdle down to the tip of the stone.

Pickle

A chemical solution used to remove oxides off a metal's surface.

Piercing

Another name given to sawing. Usually fine-toothed saw blades are used in a **piercing saw**.

Piercing saw

A jeweller's saw that holds a fine blade, taut. Available in a fixed and adjustable version.

Planishing

A technique using a hammer to flatten a metal surface.

Quench

Immersing hot metal into a solution after heating, annealing or soldering.

Ring stick

A tapered mandrel with ring sizes engraved into it and usually made of steel.

Rivet

A piece of metal to join two surfaces together.

Rouge

A polishing compound that is used as the final polish to achieve a high mirror finish.

Scribe

A sharp pointed piece of metal used to mark a line on metal. To mark out a measurement or design.

Shank

The piece of ring that encompasses the finger that does not hold the gemstone. Also called a **band**.

Solder

A metal alloy that allows the joining of two metals through heat.

Table

The top, flat facet of a gemstone – often the largest single facet of the stone – is known as the table.

Triblet

Another word for **mandrel** or former.

Work-harden

The action on a piece of metal that hardens the ability for it to bend.

INDEX

adding pips 48–49
alligator tape 11
annealing 45
apron 10
barrel polisher 24
beading tool 71, 121
bench anvil and peg 16
blades 17
borax 27
borax dish 27
brass tweezers 20
buff sticks 18
cementing 105, 109
chain ends 42
chemicals 12
claw lifter 70
collecting repairs 128
cutters 17
draw plate 25
ear protection 10
emery sticks 18
  how to make 19
findings 30–32
  bails 31
  bolt rings 81
  brooch fittings 32
  chain ends 31, 42
  trigger clasps 31, 82
  safety chains 31, 91–93
finger cots 11
finger mops 22
finger protection 11

fire extinguishers 12
first aid 10
flex shaft 21
flux 27
flux brush 27
gem ring stretcher 23, 61
gemstones 32–33
  chatons 33
  cubic zirconia 32
  garnet 33
  marcasite 33
  rubies 33
  sapphires 33
gloves 11
hand tools 16
handles 18
health and safety 10
heat insulating paste 27, 51, 54, 66, 68
hollow chains 39
how to use alligator tape 11
hypo cement 33
leather protectors 11
lemel 13
lighting 12
Liver of Sulphur 121
locating joins 45
magnetic polisher 24
magnification 20
mallet 17
metals 29
  D-section wire 29
  flat sheet 29

round wire 29
square wire 29
micro motor 21
needle files 18, 121
padlock hasp 95
pendant motor 21
plating 115–119
platinum 53, 56, 68, 112
pliers 17
polishing chains 35, 36
rings 114
polishing mops 22
polishing motor 22
precious metal reclamation 13
refinishing 111
removing stones 70
repairing
bracelets 91
chain ends 42
ear rings 85–89
figure 8 98–101
hollow chain 39
jump rings 43, 103
padlock 93–96
pear clasps 82–83
rings 45–69, 77–79
rope chain 40
simple chain 36, 104
tongue clasp 97–98
repair packets 123–127
retipping claws 73–76
reverse action tweezers 19
rhodium plating 116–118

ring clamps 18
ring file 18
riveting 85
rolling mill 21
rope chains 40
ruler 18
safety edge file 71–72
safety glasses 10
safety pickle 20, 27
saw 16
scribe 18
shank bender 23, 65
shanks 78–79
shears 17
shoes 12
smoke alarms 12
solder paste 35, 37, 40
soldering block 27
soldering boards 26
soldering surfaces 20, 26–27
steam cleaner 25
take in procedures 123
textures 120
tightening claws 71
torch 10
torches 25–26
tweezers 19
ultrasonic cleaner 24
uncollected repairs 128, 136
upright ring sizer 22, 46, 48, 59
valuations 128
workbenches 15

First published in 2026 by
The Crowood Press Ltd
Ramsbury, Marlborough
Wiltshire SN8 2HR

enquiries@crowood.com
www.crowood.com

British Library Cataloguing-in-Publication Data
A catalogue record for this book is available from the British Library.

For product safety-related questions, contact:
productsafety@crowood.com

ISBN 978 0 7198 4641 0

Legal Disclaimer
All the information provided in this book is a guide based on experience. Repairing jewellery involves the use of sharp tools and flames, and the activities carried out are potentially dangerous and hazardous, and are carried out at your own risk. The techniques carried out must be undertaken with due care, caution and diligence. We cannot be held responsible for any consequences arising from the misapplication of information, advice or instruction given in this book.

Typeset by Envisage IT
Cover design by Sergey Tsvetkov
Printed and bound in India by Thomson Press India Pvt Ltd

Dedication

This book is for, and represents, everyone who repairs jewellery.
Rarely seen but always appreciated.
We see you.

Acknowledgements

First and foremost, I would like to dedicate this book to the memory of my father, Vincent Berry. His strength, wisdom, quiet courage and his belief 'I can and I will', continue to guide me every day. His presence is deeply woven into the pages of this book, in the lessons in life he taught me, in the values he lived by, and in the love he gave so generously. I hope this book would have made him proud.

To my wife, Louise, thank you hardly seems enough. You are my rock, my sounding board and my constant encouragement through every step of this journey. Your attention to detail, thoughtful feedback, and confidence helped me shape this book into what it is. I am endlessly grateful for your patience, your love, and your belief in this project and in me. This is as much your accomplishment as it is mine.

This book would not exist without either of you. One guided my past, the other shapes my present, both inspire my future.